ENDOR
THE 7-STEP GUIDE

"This book describes critical steps often overlooked in publishing primers....I recommend this book for all authorpreneurs who are serious about creating a successful publishing venture."

BRIAN JUD, AUTHOR OF *HOW TO MAKE REAL MONEY SELLING BOOKS*, EXECUTIVE DIRECTOR OF THE ASSOCIATION OF PUBLISHERS FOR SPECIAL SALES

"Book publishing is a business but a unique type of business. Learn as much as possible by starting with this delightful read. Lots of inside detail from a successful author."

DAN POYNTER, AUTHOR OF *THE SELF PUBLISHING MANUAL*

"Very impressed by how clearly and thoroughly it walks the author through the process of publishing. Brilliant!"

BEAT BARBLAN, DIRECTOR OF BOWKER IDENTIFIER SERVICES

"*The 7-Step Guide to Authorpreneurship* is a great resource for both self-published and traditionally-published writers who are seeking a good overview to the publishing process, and want an easy-to-follow guide to publishing their book the right way. The book has simple yet effective strategies that will prove helpful for writers at all stages of their careers."

CHIP MACGREGOR, LITERARY AGENT AND OWNER OF MACGREGOR LITERARY

"By the time you've closed the back cover, you will have gained the foundational knowledge necessary to begin your career as a successful author."

K.M. WEILAND, AUTHOR OF *OUTLINING YOUR NOVEL* AND FOUNDER OF HELPINGWRITERSBECOMEAUTHORS.COM

"*I wrote a book. Now what?*' I hear this question every time I meet with a group of writers. My answer is that it's time to switch gears and start thinking like a small-business person. From now on, I will also refer them to *The 7-Step Guide to Authorpreneurship* because it is by far the most useful, straightforward guide to unlocking the mysteries of publishing and book marketing. Before you submit your writing or start down the road of self-publishing, read this book. And then read it again."

WOLF HOELSCHER, PUBMISSION FOUNDER/ PRESIDENT

"*The 7-Step Guide to Authorpreneurship* is a must-read for every author. Carter translates the concept of transitioning from hobbyist writer to career author into practical, affordable, manageable, effective strategies that can be implemented from first draft to first run."

MARIA CONNOR, AUTHOR AND FOUNDER OF
MYAUTHORCONCIERGE.COM

"Those who follow these steps *succeed*. It is truly a complete, big picture business plan for authors. I was blown away.... I have never found a single book or resource that could provide a complete picture and plan that I could recommend...until now."

LORI RISING, INTERNATIONAL BESTSELLING AUTHOR OF *WHO AM I? HOW TO DISCOVER YOUR PURPOSE AND LIVE YOUR PASSION* AND FOUNDER OF AUTHORSHIPFOREXPERTS.COM

"Rochelle Carter takes you through the ins and outs of the business like only a publishing industry veteran can. Highly recommended for new and experienced authors, PR agencies, and publishing industry executives."

BILL POTTLE, AUTHOR OF CHRISTIAN FANTASY NOVEL
ALIZEL'S SONG

"Rochelle knows this business.... Carter goes into detail in her book from the writing, editing, [and] budgeting to the launching of your book. If you skip steps, it will show! [She] pushes to make you a better author."

MELINDA TODD, AUTHOR OF *TRAILING AFTER GOD*

"After reading this book, I can now use the information that she provided for my next book. If you want to become a successful author, then you need to read this book often to learn the process of publishing your book. This book is [also] a great gift to somebody who is thinking about writing their first book [and] for those individuals that have already published their book and want to improve their knowledge."

MILTON KELLY, AUTHOR OF *WALKING IN GOD'S PATH TOWARD YOUR DESTINATION: BUILDING A PERSONAL RELATIONSHIP WITH HIM*

"This is a must read for ANYONE thinking about self-publishing or traditionally publishing a book. With all the information available it can be very confusing for new and experienced authors. This book takes the confusion out and walks you through each step of a successful book launch. Amazing and a breath of fresh air."

SARAH DEW, BUSINESS STRATEGIST AND PRODUCTIVITY EXPERT AT THE HAPPY ENTREPRENEUR

"As an author and owner of a literary services company, I'm often asked about resources I would recommend. *The 7-Step Guide to Authorpreneurship* by Rochelle Carter will be placed on the top of my reading list for authors. Carter expertly guides the author through the publishing process, developing a business plan, building a platform and so much more. This is a comprehensive guide on the business of writing that I believe all authors should have in their library."

TYORA MOODY, AUTHOR AND LITERARY ENTREPRENEUR

PLAN · WRITE · PUBLISH ·

THE
SEVEN STEP
GUIDE
TO

AUTHORPRENEURSHIP

ROCHELLE CARTER
Edited By VERONIKA WALKER

EVERFAITH PRESS

Copyright © 2013 by Rochelle D. Carter
2014 EverFaith Press Edition

The 7-Step Guide to Authorpreneurship/ Carter, Rochelle D.

Paperback ISBN: 978-1937844745
eBook ISBN: 978-1937844707
Library of Congress Control Number: 2013951674

Ellechor Media, LLC
EverFaith Press Imprint
1915 NW Amberglen Pkwy, Suite 400
Beaverton, OR 97006

www.everfaithpress.com

DEDICATION

This book is dedicated with love to my two daughters:

Al-Naiyel Amadi Naysa, my Royal Vessel and Joyful Miracle of God

Al-Rielle Khali Amara, my Fierce, Graceful, Golden Lioness of God

May you always have the wisdom to know what brings you joy, and the strength to chase after it!

TABLE OF CONTENTS

Dedication. 7

Table Of Contents 9

Foreword By Author K.M. Weiland 13

Foreword By Beat Barblan,
Director Of Bowker Identifier Services 17

Introduction: Authorpreneurship 101. 21

Step 1: Write And Polish Your Manuscript 27

    Write Your Book Summary. 29

    Edit Your Book. 32

    Hire An Editor 38

Step 2: Create Your Business Plan 49

    Your Power Team
    (Aka The Author Super-Group) 49

    Business Plan Elements 55

    Budget First. 55

    Simple Book Marketing Budget 57

    Time To Strategize 58

    Suggested Publishing Timeline 60

    Executive Summary 63

Step 3: Create Your Author Platform 65

    What Is A Book Marketing Plan?. 66

    Get Started Early:
    Research The Book Market. 67

Five Essential Elements To Start
Your Marketing Plan 68

Your Author Platform 71

Step 4: Engage Your Audience 89

Social Media: The Self-Promotion Toolkit 103

Keep Up With Everyone 114

Step 5: Get Ready To Launch 119

Your Press Release 120

Requesting Interviews 121

Soliciting Early Reviews. 127

Pre-Launch Event 130

Throw A Book Launch Party 132

Get Your Book In Bookstores 141

Step 6: Keep The Momentum 149

Post-Launch Strategies 150

Rethink Book Tours. 156

Book Buy Bomb (aka "Buy My Book Day") . . . 159

Attend Local Fairs & Events. 161

Step 7: Pay It Forward 163

Cross Promotion Rules & Benefits. 165

Create Your Campaign. 167

Design The Timeline 168

Coordinate Your Materials 168

Create Your Pre-Launch Page And Follow-Ups. 169

Create Promo Copy 170

Create Clear Instructions. 171

Blind Date With A Book 171

Your Own Bookshop 173

Conclusion 175

 Questions To Always Ask Yourself 175

 One Last Word On Marketing 176

 ...And One On Your Author Brand 177

 Next Steps 178

Bibliography 181

Appendix A. Book Reviewers 185

Appendix B. eBook Promotional Sites 193

Appendix C. Fairs, Tradeshows,
Conventions & Conferences. 197

Appendix D. Sample Letters & Templates. 201

 Book Review/Author Interview Request Sample . 201

 Endorsement Request Template 205

Additional Resources 207

Acknowledgements 209

About The Author 211

FOREWORD

AUTHOR K.M. WEILAND

I NEVER WANTED TO be an author. A writer, you bet. But not an author—because being an author seemed to mean doing a whole lot more than just threading my fantasies across the page, one lovely black-and-white word at time. Being an *author* meant selling my books. It meant becoming someone who had to be brave, chatty, professional, socially competent, business-savvy, and relentlessly ambitious.

But that wasn't me. I was introverted, shy, and content to live in my ivory tower. I didn't even like talking on the phone. How was I supposed to transform myself into this author person—this *businessperson*—who hawked books, came up with marketing plans, and made a living off her writing? I was a *writer*; I knew nothing about business and marketing. And, what's more, I didn't want to know.

What I *did* want was for readers to buy my books. The publication date for my second novel, a historical set during the Middle Ages, was fast approaching, and

I wanted it to be a success. Or, if it couldn't succeed, I at least wanted to go down knowing I had done everything in my power to *try* to make it a success. If that meant learning a little bit about marketing, so be it.

I joined Facebook and Twitter. I started promoting my website "Helping Writers Become Authors." I planned a book launch. I printed bookmarks. I even pretended to be that chatty professional long enough to hawk the novel at every bookshop in town.

It was scary. Sometimes it was a little bewildering. But, shockingly, somewhere along the way, I realized it was something else as well: it was empowering.

As time went by I began to invest as much time in my business skills as I always had in my writing skills. My book sales slowly picked up. My blog and social media followings grew. A few years later I published another book—the non-fiction how-to *Outlining Your Novel: Map Your Way to Success*. Within its first week in the Kindle store, it climbed to #1 in the Writing Skills category, held that spot for over a year, and even still remains in the top ten. My next novel, the fantasy *Dreamlander*, hit #1 in its category in the first *day*, and my next how-to book, *Structuring Your Novel*, sits right on top of *Outlining Your Novel* in the rankings.

Suddenly, I wasn't just a writer anymore. I was a full-time author. But, more than that, I was an *authorpreneur*.

In the introduction to this book Rochelle says, "The only way to get your book noticed the way *you* want it to be is to invest in yourself." *Yourself*, not the book.

What writer doesn't want to be able to write full-time? Quitting the day job is something we all dream about at one point or another. We want to support ourselves and our families doing the thing we love. But to do that, we have to do more than pursue excellence in our writing. We have to take on the entrepreneurial mindset and relish it.

In the pages of this book, Rochelle teaches you how to do that. If you're like I was, back when I was trying to figure out how to promote that second novel, then you may be willing to do what it takes, but you probably have little or no idea where to start. What does it take to be an authorpreneur? Where will you find your audience? How will you approach them? How will you avoid gaffes that will tarnish your professionalism? How will you create your platform and, even more importantly, how will you create a long-term business plan that will sustain your dreams of a writing-centric lifestyle for years to come?

If you've found yourself asking any of those questions, then the book you're holding is the perfect place to start in your quest for the answers. By the time you've closed the back cover you will have gained the foundational knowledge necessary to begin your career as a successful author. You will have learned about this brave new world of publishing we've entered into in the 21st century, and you will have been introduced to the tremendous possibilities and opportunities that await you if you're willing to do whatever it takes to succeed.

Remember that person I was convinced I could never be? As this crazy writing-publishing-marketing journey progresses, I've found myself stepping into her shoes a little more every day. My biggest success isn't the number of books I've sold, but the personal empowerment I've gained along the way. These days, when people ask me what I do for a living, I don't tell them I'm a writer—I tell them I'm an *author*. And you can too!

K.M. Weiland
Internationally Published, Best-selling
Author and Writing Coach
www.kmweiland.com
www.helpingwritersbecomeauthors.com

FOREWORD

BEAT BARBLAN, DIRECTOR OF BOWKER IDENTIFIER SERVICES

A FEW YEARS AGO a flurry of calls started to come in to the ISBN Agency here at Bowker. While specifics differed, the theme of the callers was the same. The person on the other end of the line would be an author who had written a great book, but sales were not picking up. Could we help? At that time, while we encouraged writers to submit good title data that we would collect and distribute throughout the supply chain, there wasn't much we could do. We were unsure of what would be most useful to the writer. Clearly here was a broad need and an opportunity that wanted fulfilling.

In recent years, with the advent of digital publishing and decreased costs for Print On Demand, more and more authors have pursued the option of publishing their titles independently. Perhaps out of frustration with finding a publisher to take them on, a desire for higher payments, or the sheer excitement of embarking on an entrepreneurial adventure where they retain total control of their book projects, a growing number of authors have decided to take matters into their own hands. It was time for Bowker to go to work and start exploring this space to identify what pain-points authors were facing and what would be helpful to them. We read surveys, talked to authors and small publishing houses, scoured the web for information and organizations, and attended national and international conferences. We gathered large amounts of data on the new trends in publishing, particularly about what is commonly referred to as "self-publishing." We also discovered that while a lot of information is available, much of it is scattered in a vast, jumbled universe, making it impossible for an independent author to find quick and clear answers.

One thing we discovered almost immediately is that there is no such thing as "self-publishing." Publishing is always a collective effort, and no single individual, no matter how immersed in the field, can complete it alone. Be it printing, shipping, converting to an eBook, marketing, distributing, editing, designing, or maintaining a visible and relevant social presence, somewhere along the publishing process, even the most determined and independently-minded author will likely need some help publishing her book.

Publishing, it turns out, is a complex process under the best of circumstances and even when the writer works with an established publisher. No author, independent or contracted, can write a manuscript, hand it over to some entity, and wait for the checks to roll in. Even the most successful writers have to stay constantly engaged. These select few may have great editors and may duck the worries over eBook conversion, distribution, or printing, but they will very likely be involved in marketing and publicity. They will keep their presence on social networks fresh and exciting, participate in events at bookstores and conferences, conduct interviews, blog about their latest work, go to book signing parties, and generally take an active role in their project.

While conducting our research, we began to recognize a common profile of an author who seemed consistently more successful than others. This is the author that Rochelle Carter, in her wonderfully clear and straightforward book, *The 7-Step Guide to Authorpreneurship,* calls the "authorpreneur." She defines "authorpreneur" as "an author who is not just creative, but also a business person who works for him- or herself."

I love how Rochelle's book is pragmatic, to the point, and critical for any author who wants to take full control—or even just more control—over the success of her book. Describing the publishing process in a way that is simple to understand is not an easy task. But it is one that Rochelle achieves beautifully, bringing the author up to speed with essential, logically presented, and organized information quickly and painlessly.

Her approach is refreshing and thorough, free from numbing minutiae or boring lectures. Rochelle is the rare teacher who engages her students in a participatory class from which they will leave well informed, more mature, and with the necessary tools to succeed.

Ms. Carter walks her reader through every essential step, from writing the manuscript to creating a marketing campaign for the book, providing easy-to-follow instructions and guidelines on such critical components as developing a budget and a business plan, engaging the audience, and publishing a press release. She leaves no step uncovered, all the while offering valuable tidbits of information for authors at any level and with diverse needs. *The 7-Step Guide to Authorpreneurship* is essential reading not only for the "self-publisher" but also for any author who wants to take the next step and become a truly successful author, i.e. an authorpreneur!

BEAT BARBLAN
DIRECTOR, BOWKER IDENTIFIER SERVICES
WWW.BOWKER.COM

INTRODUCTION

AUTHORPRENEURSHIP 101

S O, YOU'RE WRITING or have written a book that you think everyone should know about. You've gone through the steps and tried to find an agent or publisher who will fund your dream and spread your message to the world. But now—whether you've just been rejected for the hundredth time, or whether you've finally gotten your manuscript published but are quickly becoming disillusioned with the whole process and are suffering from a nonexistent support system—you are wallowing in business lingo, financial pressures, and lack of success.

"We've done all we can, your publisher says. Money is tight. You're good, but we just don't have the time or money to get the results you're asking for." Or you look at your sales of your first eBook...and it's still the same single-digit number as last month.

This is *not* how you imagined your writing career would turn out.

I'm going to share a little secret with you, no charge:

The only way to get your book noticed the way you want it to be is to invest in yourself.

Sounds odd, perhaps. Invest in myself, not in my book?

Well, the secret is that by investing in yourself as an entire person, you're going to be investing in your book as well. You can't just sell an idea or a book to a publisher or audience—you have to sell yourself as well.

How do you do that, you ask?

You become what is termed an "authorpreneur": an author who is not just a creative but also a business-person who works for him- or herself.

"Authorpreneur" is not just the new catch-name of the season. It speaks to the state of mind that you need to have before, during, and even after you have a book released. It doesn't matter if you decide to publish independently (go "indie") or traditionally, or if you want to handle marketing for the book on your own or hire a publicist instead. The mindset is still the same: *you* are determining and handling your writing career— your way.

Michael Flowers, author of *Creative Writing and Authorpreneurship*, calls authorpreneurship "the art of translating your writing ability into a stream of income." Kris Tualla, author of *Becoming an Authorpreneur*, says an authorpreneur is an "author who creates a written product, participates in creating their own brand, and actively promotes that brand through a variety of outlets."

No matter what definition you prefer, the result is *an entrepreneur who, recognizing his or her own talent in writing, has successfully turned that talent into a business.*

As a veteran book publisher and project manager with both traditional and self-publishing imprints, I have found that the weaknesses of most authors come in similar formats. The authors' mindsets revolve around their (often limited) understanding of the publishing industry, which in turn results in their either taking too little ownership of their book and brand, or too much ownership when team strategy should be the priority.

In an effort to provide a substantial guide for authors who are doing things on their own, I have scoured the Internet and talked with various experts and professional authors to gather the most tried and true, effective, smart, and *affordable* ways for a new author to plan their publication and sell more books. I personally believe that *smart money makes money,* and while you may have to spend a little to get a book published and printed, you should also know where your money is going and how to strategically use your budget where it will profit you the most...without wasting your time on not having a strategy at all or having ones that won't provide a good return for you. (Hiring a publicist is not a bad idea, but only consider that option *after* you have laid the groundwork discussed in this book.)

Do not think for one second that being an authorpreneur is *just* about writing books! To be profitable at your highest degree, you will need to diversify, offering not just books but audio tapes, training on topics you have built your brand on, speaking engagements, apps, etc. But to keep things simple, this book focuses solely on the book-publishing journey of an authorpreneur.

WHO THIS BOOK IS FOR

If you are looking for a book discussing the benefits of social media and self-publishing, seeking to convince you that it is the wave of the future—and the only method any sane person should consider for publishing—this is not the book for you. Although most of the material here is applicable to that industry, I am not here to simply jump on the self-publishing, indie bandwagon.

On the other hand, I'm not advocating traditional publishing alone, either. Each industry has its merits, and as I have experience in both arenas, I know it simply boils down to which route the author wants to take. The beauty of authorpreneurship, once again, is: it's all up to you.

If, however, you are searching for a literal guide to planning your book, building your social media presence and platform, launching your first publication to an awaiting audience, and seeing the industry from a business-minded standpoint, then this *is* the book for you. I have outlined a clear path for you, from planning your book and finishing the manuscript to publishing either as an indie or traditional author, establishing your online presence, and launching your release. If you have already published your book you may find you do not need to read each step, so you can skip around to find the steps that address your current struggles. I would still advise reading the entire book through once first so you can be accurately informed of all the tools and resources available to you...and perhaps make it easier on yourself as you write your next book!

YOU'VE BEEN WARNED...

I have to warn you: you have to be ready to work when you read this book. It can take up to two or three months to properly set these tools up and follow the advice offered here. If you really want the writing career you've always dreamed about, then hard work must go hand-in-hand with your writing passion. You'll find the rewards to be more than worth the labor-intensive next few months.

So, are you ready to begin?
Ready to work?
Ready to sell more books?

Then let's get started.

STEP 1

WRITE AND POLISH YOUR MANUSCRIPT

ONE OF THE hardest parts of becoming an author is writing. Not everyone is cut out for it.

It's also the first and most important step to becoming an authorpreneur, so it's vital that you analyze your current desires and make sure that you have what it takes to be a professional, business-minded author.

Do you "dabble"? Professional authors don't get that way by writing a sentence or two here or there—they put hours and hours of work into each project and manuscript, then edit their work (more than once!) through critique groups and professional editors…and then they start writing their next book.

If you prefer to write little works here or there, or simply want to write some short pieces just for the fun of it, you may not be an authorpreneur in the way this book defines it. You enjoy writing for writing's sake, but you consider it more of a hobby than a business venture. There's nothing wrong with that. Enjoy your creativity and have fun unencumbered with business plans and contracts.

If you want to make more than a few pennies off your work, though, you're going to need to refocus your energies on creating content that audiences will want to read and that publishers want to publish. This kind of content only comes through days, weeks, and months of long, hard work that is cultivated by market knowledge of the subject or genre you're writing in.

Planning your short story collection, nonfiction work, or full-length novel for success includes:

1. **Deciding on your genre or topic.** Do you want to write fiction, nonfiction, or a hybrid known as creative nonfiction? If fiction, will it be fantasy, sci-fi, historical, or romance? If nonfiction, is it a biography, documentary, self-help, or inspirational topic?

2. **Deciding on the subject, or the main character and plotline.** Who is the book about? What is the problem they have to solve, or what does the reader need to know about the subject in a nonfiction work?

3. **Working out a satisfying hook and resolution.** What is the "hook," the action that will compel your readers to keep reading? What is the resolution, or the ending that makes all the threads come together and satisfies the

reader? What is the call-to-action in your nonfiction work, or the overall goal you want to bring to your readers' attention?

If you haven't finished your draft yet, use the above points to get started in your planning. If you are already well into your draft, just take some time to think about and implement these questions into your story for a cohesive, well laid-out manuscript.

It doesn't help you to read through the guidance in this book if you don't have a book to sell yet! So, before you do anything else...go finish that first draft.

Then come back to this chapter when you're done.

WRITE YOUR BOOK SUMMARY

Okay, now that you've finished writing your first draft (you *are* finished, aren't you? No cheating, now!), it's good to write out a general summary—also known as a "blurb"—of your novel or nonfiction work. It will help your potential readers to know what the book is about, as well as help you ensure that your story or topic actually delivers on what your blurb promises. It's also helpful in preparing for and getting the attention of an editor or agent.

And guess what? Writing your book summary is your first marketing task! Even if the book is not edited or market-ready yet, the book summary is essential for drumming up attention for your book. Use the book summary on the back cover of your book, on the websites of bookstores, and on your personal website. Whenever your book is mentioned, it should be included if possible!

As you begin writing your book summary, be aware that the tone of the summary is and should be very different from the writing style you developed in the actual book itself. Marketing language is different from fiction or nonfiction prose. Its goal is different, too: marketing language is seeking to grab a potential reader's attention and make him or her want to read the actual book. Think of it like a commercial—you have to make your product look interesting enough to buy, and you aren't given much time to convince your audience that it's worth it.

A few tips to get you started:

- **Give the reader just a taste.** You are trying to convey a feeling or tone, or are promising an answer to a problem, but not offering too many details. The book itself will take care of that.

- **Compel them to read further by focusing on only one clear benefit or outcome.** Even though you may want to list a whole slew of reasons why a reader should buy your book, resist the urge. You can overwhelm your customers very quickly with too many promises, rather than hooking them with just one. This goes hand-in-hand with the next point....

- **Write to a specific reader.** Potential readers honestly aren't interested in why you wrote the book, whether it's to fulfill a lifelong dream or expose an awful truth. They want to know what's in it for them and why they should care. How does your blurb address your specific reader? What type of language and tone will capture their attention? A businessperson will respond to a certain marketing tone that a homemaker or teenager wouldn't. Imagine the reader you want to read your books, and talk to *them*.

- **Cut out the fluff.** This is the over-arching theme I want to leave with you. Your natural inclination will be to add more, tell more, and show more. Resist the urge and try cutting instead. What can you get rid of while still conveying your point? If it doesn't absolutely have to be there, cut it to better relate to consumers' very short attention spans. Remember, readers are bombarded with hundreds of books screaming at them from the shelves to "read me!" The books with blurbs that are easy to grasp without complicated paragraphs and superfluous lingo have a better chance of being bought. Short sentences that read more like bullet points or that summarize the story quickly will help your reader make a quick decision. A good length is about 100–175 words. You may still be asked to shorten it even more, but this is a great word count to help you "cut out the fluff."

EDIT YOUR BOOK

Okay, so now you've finished your draft and have written a short, punchy summary of your book that is sure to catch a potential reader's eye. Now…the real work begins.

It's time to get that manuscript publish-ready by beginning the editing process.

Begin with a basic self-edit where you re-read your manuscript and make any necessary changes or add scenes that you missed when you wrote the first draft. Be as thorough as you can by reading your entire manuscript carefully and making sure it all flows together smoothly. ***Do not spend more than two weeks editing on your own.*** Why? Because after two weeks, you are either just wasting time playing with phrases or punctuation, or you are procrastinating and not doing much work on it, anyway. Either way, it's time to move on!

Beta-readers

After you have completed a basic first edit on your own, it's time to find some "beta-readers."

A beta-reader is someone who you believe fits into the demographic (age, race, sex, profession, and salary bracket) you think would be most interested in reading your book. You should look at your book's central focus, characters, topic, and overall message to help you narrow this down. Understand the problems that you solve with your publication.

Now you need to paint a picture of the ideal reader. For instance: who, broadly speaking, reads self-help books about depression, leadership, children, etc.? Who reads young adult books? Who reads books with supernatural elements or highly literary language? Do some research on your genre and/or topic and find out the general type of person who might be interested in your book's theme, genre, or character types. Define them in as many relevant ways as possible, and try to focus on who will gain the most value from your book.

Once you've determined this demographic and found a few people who fit in it (try writers who blog, online writing forums like CritiqueCircle.com, or face-to-face writing groups), send them a polite, well-edited request for a critique. Ideally you'll want two or three people's feedback for a well-rounded idea of how well you are conveying your ideas or hooking your readers.

Be prepared for negative feedback! It may be that you have improperly selected your demographic, that certain themes or characters just don't resonate well with an individual, or that they don't know how to effectively point out the good as well as the bad. Just be ready to take the feedback with a grain of salt and look for the constructive criticisms that beta-readers offer, even if they don't say it well.

It may be helpful to use a survey tool like Zoomerang, SurveyMonkey, or even Google Forms like the one I did here (http://bit.ly/ReaderFeedbackForm) to get feedback from your beta-readers, depending on your method of communication. You can copy and re-use my template, or create your own. Try asking questions like these, using a scale from 1-5 to ask your reviewers whether the following is true:

1. I enjoyed the topic/plot of this book

2. I related to or felt appropriate connections to the characters in this book

3. I related to the topic (or the main character's conflict, if fiction) and felt it was important

4. I enjoyed the format of this book

5. I enjoyed the prose style/dialogue of this book

6. I felt the author was knowledgeable of the subject and I trusted their credibility

7. Additional comments and suggestions (What was the book missing? How can the author improve the story or style? What else would you want the author to know about your reading experience?)

After you have received sufficient feedback, reassess your demographic and seek to incorporate the suggestions you received into your manuscript by adding, deleting, or rewriting sections as needed. Keep in mind your beta-readers may contradict each other, so be sure to look for the credibility of what each individual said—and remember to not take it personally!

Beta-editor

"Beta-editor" is a term exclusive to this book. I feel it necessary to distinguish between the first editor who looks at your book and the editor who will actually lead you into publication. Your beta-editor, while qualified to be a final editor as well, is one who works on your book with one specific goal in mind: to ensure that it is readable, organized, and logical with seamless transitions and pacing. A beta-editor is *not* your local English teacher or your buddy who writes well. Unless they have tangible experience editing the type of book you have written, they are not qualified and, while well-intentioned, may steer you very wrong. Consider them as a beta-reader for more general feedback, but you can find your beta-editor by talking to other authors or posting online on Elance, Craigslist, or MediaBistro. I have also heard some authors use Edit911 and EditFast.com, and self-publishing companies like my imprint EverFaith Press will have their own editors on staff if you hire them to do your initial editing.

Your beta-editor takes the same approach as your beta-readers, but has the experience and credentials to offer professional advice on how to reorganize, rewrite, and streamline your story and narrative so that it reads well. You should seek an editor who has experience with *developmental editing*. A *developmental editor* is:

> *A person who deals with the overall organization of a manuscript rather than with changes such as wording of sentences or punctuation. A developmental editor also addresses reordering of entire blocks of text or entire chapters. The edit may also address tone, voice, addition or deletion of material, complexity of material, and transitions among paragraphs and sections of the manuscript.*

The developmental editor may or may not correct grammar and spelling along the way, but that's not where you want to spend time so early on in the process. Make sure your beta-editor knows that your goal is to have an organized, easy-to-read manuscript with a solid story from beginning to end, and that this is a priority *above* seeking someone who will offer you detailed grammatical editing. Many developmental editors will implement their advice with a service known as "manuscript critiquing," in which they provide you with detailed comments and suggestions for restructuring plot points that don't flow well, improving character development and world building, and structuring theories and arguments in a more logical, concise way.

Remember that your beta-editor may be the editor who helps you continue on to publication, but that is your choice. You may want another editor to help you during the second stage (see below) for even more advice and guidance.

Once you have received a manuscript critique and/or other services with the beta-editor, implement his or her suggestions through rewrites and additions. This is your rewriting stage, and should be taken seriously. This is where your manuscript really starts to shine. Take as long as you need to polish your manuscript and make sure that you are happy with your work. You may—and probably will—do more edits in the future, but the bulk of the story, theme, and impression your readers will have are solidified in this stage—so take your time!

When you're finally done with your rewrites, I recommend you do one more self-editing pass before putting space between yourself and the manuscript. During this editing pass:

1. **Read the manuscript from back to front, chapter by chapter.** Each chapter is a mini-story all its own, and reading them separate from the rest of the manuscript will help

you analyze whether you and your beta-editor accomplished the task of developing a well-organized, solid manuscript.

2. **Print and read your manuscript out loud.** When you force yourself to read each chapter aloud, you will notice misspellings, typos, or awkward phrases that your eyes glossed over before. You may not want to read the entire manuscript, but at least read the first, middle, and final chapter.

3. **Put it away!**

Once again, do not spend more than two weeks on this second self-editing phase. You have spent a lot of time on your manuscript at this point, so you need to force yourself to move on. It is time to put space between you and the manuscript so you can revisit it later with fresh and more critical eyes.

HIRE AN EDITOR

Okay, so at this point, after three to four weeks of *not* looking at your manuscript (yes, three to four weeks. Trust me.), you should be ready for the second phase of professional editing. You're ready to put the final polish on the manuscript and buff it up so that it will attract a publishing agent's eye, or meet the quality expectations of your eager audience if you're self-publishing.

There are several things to consider in hiring a second editor to help you in this phase.

Determine The Type Of Editing You Need

First, clarify what kind of assistance you're seeking. Does your manuscript need a substantive edit to work out kinks in the story, a copy edit, or proofreading?

Substantive editing involves intensive attention to plotting, narrative, characterization, tone, and other holistic factors for fiction, as well as logic, flow, and effective messaging in nonfiction. If your novel has been rejected for publication or your nonfiction lacks the impact it requires, you should search for an editor who performs substantive editing. Again, this could be the beta-editor you worked with before, or you may choose to find a new editor with fresh eyes and ideas. It's up to you.

If you feel the plot and organization are sound but that the narrative needs more energy and punch, or if you are concerned it may be clunky and awkward at the sentence level, look for an editor who specializes in *line editing. Line editors* specialize in developing an author's voice and style, and enhancing unique qualities and recognizable traits of an author's "sound" by focusing on the tone and flow of the narrative sentence by sentence. In other words, line editors help enhance the parts of your writing voice that make you recognizably *you*.

If you think the content and narrative are in good

shape and believe you just need a revision for grammar, usage, and punctuation, find a *copy editor*; if you're only concerned about typographical errors and final cleanup, hire a *proofreader.*

Note that many editors offer several or all of these services, so be sure to ask what their range, experience, and abilities are. If you're lucky, you may find an editor who can provide the whole bundle for you at a good rate, or you may decide you want several different editors of various skillsets. Once again, it's all up to you!

Search For An Editor

Now the question is…where exactly do you *find* an editor? There are a variety of ways to go about this, so you should experiment and see what works for you.

Many authors' first instinct is to post physical or virtual notes in their community to solicit local teachers or graduate students with English majors. Though these may be economical choices, teachers and grad students do not necessarily always make good editors unless they specialize in editing manuscripts. Oftentimes, their main concern is reading for literary quality and merit, and they may struggle with editing your manuscript with *your specific audience* in mind. An English major or professor trained in analyzing British literature of the 18th century, for instance, will struggle to identify the needs your romance or fantasy novel may have, because the audiences and expectations of those genres are entirely different from what the English major works with every day of his or her life. If you're going to hire a professor or graduate student to edit your manuscript, get picky. Find someone who deals with your genre specifically in their daily work—for example, a creative writing professor would be ideal for fiction writers—to ensure that they intrinsically understand who your audience is and can help you craft the manuscript accordingly.

You can also put projects up for bid on websites like Elance or Guru. Be warned, however: this is often a complicated process, and many editors on these sites may be under-qualified or not proficient in American or British English. Also, if you lowball the rate range that you're willing to pay...you'll get what you paid for.

Employment sites such as MediaBistro are often effective for finding publishing and media professionals, but not so much for obtaining help with fiction projects or small-scale assignments like short story or essay collections. Posting employment listings can also be pricey, and the responses more difficult to wade through.

Craigslist, however, remains an excellent source. Job postings cost only $75, and you don't need to restrict your search to your local area. In addition, organizations such as the Bay Area Editor's Forum or the Editors Freelance Association are appropriate resources for private individuals and smaller businesses seeking editorial assistance. There are many discussion forums on LinkedIn groups as well where you can post a call for editors.

Alternatively, many freelance editors advertise their services on their own websites. Just run a Google search and do your research on each. Once again, geographic location is largely irrelevant.

One of the best methods is to either work through a self-publishing press, such as EverFaith Press, that provides stand-alone editorial support, or get a recommendation for a freelance editor (often called a "book doctor") from a successfully published author. Both options have their advantages and disadvantages, of course. Self-publishing presses don't let you choose the specific editor you work with, while you can choose a freelance editor at will. On the other hand, freelance editors don't always provide you with a wide breadth of publishing knowledge or additional book cover and typesetting services that self-publishing presses do. Editors are also not—I repeat: *not*—literary agents, and will not represent you to a publishing house.

Freelance Editing Budget

Your biggest question at this point is probably how much all this will cost. Self-publishing presses and editors both vary in how they handle cost, and it can get pricey, but the return on the investment is well worth it.

Developmental and substantive editing services usually run around $50 or more per hour, and the typical working rate is several pages per hour. Line and copy editors charge anywhere from $25 to $50 per hour, depending on their level of experience and expertise on the subject matter, and the shape the manuscript is in when they get it. They generally complete five to ten pages an hour.

Proofreading usually costs less and is accomplished more quickly, but unless the content is online or you don't mind receiving electronic copies, proofreaders often mail proofs, send them as a PDF document (the editor will need a special editing program), or complete the project on site and pick up and deliver upon completion.

If you feel you can only afford a limited amount of editing, sacrifice substantive and line editing for copy editing and proofreading. Your beta-readers and beta-editor have been able to help you refine your plot and character development and perhaps your dialogue and sentence structure, but a book that has not been copy edited and proofread is always at risk of being substandard (and it almost always is). It is the quickest turn-off for your readers and potential agents reading your sample if the pages are riddled with typos and missing punctuation.

You can test the waters by asking a potential editor or self-publishing press for a sample edit before committing to them. In fact, it's a good idea in order to make sure that the editor understands your purpose and goals, that their method and style of editing is helpful and communicated effectively, and that (in your opinion) they're worth what they charge. Some editors offer free samples while others may charge you a few dollars, but both are viable options. Be sure to check out their testimonials and references if you're on the fence about them.

On a side note, while many freelance editors charge per hour as explained above, some like to use a flat rate (or a combination of hourly plus a flat fee) based on the entire project length and needs. Flat rates include not just the work on the manuscript, but also any conference calls, emails, research, or additional resources needed. There is no set way that freelance editors charge, so just discuss their particular method and see what works for both of you.

Be sure to ask *how* your potential editor or self-publishing press accepts payment. Is it by check, money order, PayPal, or other electronic service? Most freelance editors will ask for a percentage of the total cost upfront and/or after you receive a specific portion of the edited material. Again, make sure you ask the editor to complete a sample edit of a few pages so that you can evaluate their methods and work style before approving them.

As you can see, hiring an editor or press service is an expensive proposition. Engaging even a $25-per-hour copy editor for a 100,000-word novel will cost you about a thousand dollars. An experienced substantive editor could end up billing you a few hundred dollars for helping you craft a 2,500-word article, or a few thousand dollars for helping you streamline your novel's plot holes. Even having some web pages proofread can easily become a three-figure expense.

Nevertheless, consider the result: a literary agent is impressed with your snappy, engaging prose. A reader writes a rave review that pumps your book into a top listing on Amazon. Your typo-free website, which your proofreader has also improved with apt suggestions about format and design, attracts hundreds of new visitors who increase your turnover rate, boost sales, and create readers. It's nearly impossible to quantify the effect an editorial professional's contribution has on your content—and your reputation as a professional (the essence of a true authorpreneur).

Moreover, editors often become authors' loudest advocates and cheerleaders as they begin their book launch or start contacting agents. Your editor spends almost as much time with your book as you do by the time they're done with it, and their goal is to help you enhance and make your manuscript even better than it was before. They *want* you to succeed. Having an editor at your side can really help you through any discouragement or doubts you have as you begin (and continue) your publishing journey. So consider that you're not just getting a service when you hire an editor, but often a consultant and mentor for your publishing journey as well.

Sure, it's a leap of faith to hire a service or editor,

in many ways. There's no guaranteeing that employing a certain editor (even one armed with an impressive resume or glowing testimonials) will result in publication or a successful career-boost. The process of obtaining the right editor and publishing service isn't effortless, even in the best circumstances. It takes hard work and an acute sense of professionalism—and a lot of patience. However, if you're willing to put in the time, you'll reap the benefits soon enough, and you (and your readers) will be so glad you did.

Interview Potential Editors

This particular step may seem daunting, but it is important that your editor is both qualified on paper and also compatible in person and/or virtually. The action needed here is simple: get to know the editor you think is a good fit. Below are five basic questions, and as you talk with the editor, pay attention to the answers while determining if their attitude and ability to communicate works for you.

1. **How many years of experience do you have editing [book genre]?** The genre portion is especially important, because an editor with 30 years of non-fiction editing experience may not be the best fit for a fantasy novel.

2. **How would you handle sensitive writers who question every edit you make?** You need a thick skin in the editing process, but you also want an honest editor with tact and integrity. He or she should be able to kindly tell you the truth *and* work with you, not give up if you don't agree.

3. **What is your familiarity with InDesign and Quark? Are you familiar with any other page layout software?** This answer will let you know if the editor is able to help you with interior layout in the final print stage, or if they will be able to edit once a designer has put the book interior together. Not required, but nice to have if you are on a budget!

4. **There are two projects with the same deadline. One client is easygoing while the other constantly calls to ask when we will be done. Which project do you make your top priority?** If you are a laid-back soul, this is a critical question. You may not like confrontation, but you need an editor to show integrity and an ability to properly multi-task. Hint: The correct answer is that they do their best to complete both projects on time.

5. **Why should I hire you as my editor?**
   No right or wrong answer here, so you be the judge. Are they sincere? Experienced? Affordable? Likeable? If all of these answers are yes, you may have a winner.

STEP 2

CREATE YOUR BUSINESS PLAN

A S AN AUTHOR, your dream is to not only see your book in print, but for it to touch as many lives as possible, right?

For the true authorpreneur, however, you are seeking to touch lives *and* to make a profit with your book. No matter the subject or genre, your book is your contribution to society. This is why you have to treat it as a *business*. And of course, every business needs a business *plan*.

YOUR POWER TEAM (AKA THE AUTHOR SUPER-GROUP)

The first thing anyone needs before they create a business plan is a network, and an author is no different. I'm not talking about a marketing platform focused on getting readers (that comes later, in chapter 3). When I say "network," I mean a handpicked community of experts and fellow authorpreneurs you've chosen to help you learn about, study, and flourish in the publishing industry.

These individuals are your "author super-group." Think of them as your "power team."

Your super-group is comprised of individuals and/or businesses with whom you share common goals or audiences. These members can help you improve your publishing strategy, identify more marketing opportunities, hone your message, expand your reach, and connect with more readers.

Keep in mind that many of the individuals and companies who qualify for your super-group will charge for their time. The savvy authorpreneur will seek out ones who are willing to impart their knowledge in free consultations or personal exchanges. You should only pay for someone's services once you fully understand your own limitations and how they can be supplemented through the help of someone more experienced in that particular area. You should also have an idea of some of the tactics this person will use in order to clearly deliver what he or she promises. Hiring someone before you build up your own publishing knowledge and establish some sort of acquaintanceship with that individual can end in disaster, and often leaves you dissatisfied...and out a lot of money.

I personally sought out self-proclaimed gurus for various services when I was starting out, and the biggest problem I saw was that if I didn't know what to ask for, they could not provide me with what I needed. This means that until you can efficiently state your specific needs for them and outline your idea of what success looks like, you are wasting your time and, most importantly, your money. Figure out what works for you, what doesn't, and where you want to spend your time in your regular business day.

Another way to look at it is to put yourself in other people's shoes. What would you like if roles were reversed? What would a blogger want? If you can bring them enough traffic and engaged readers, they will be very interested in helping you promote or give away your book. As the Zig Ziglar quote says, "You can have whatever you want in life if you help enough other people get what they want." Don't be the one giving bad experiences and wasting other people's time or money. Be productive—helping your team is your second job.

Key members of an author super-group include:

- **Industry professionals** – No matter the topic or theme of your book, there will always be some mover or shaker who already commands a strong following in that same area. These could be novelists with a specific readership or message (like authors focusing on high school culture or abusive relationships), or experts on your nonfiction topic like Middle Eastern politics, genetics research, or business leadership. Seek out these individuals through their websites and contact info and seek to cultivate a relationship with them. They're connected, and know what your readers are looking for. They might be able to get you into events and speaking engagements that will put you directly in front of your target audience, because you share the same one.

- **Other authors in your genre** – Wait, they're your competition, right? Not necessarily. If you have differentiated yourself well, your work will stand out when compared to other authors' work. Each author has something unique to give to his or her readers, but authors in the same genre (like the industry gurus) share the same audience and market to the same people. As you begin to grow your platform and market your book (Step 3: Create Your Author Platform), you should begin developing a following, and one way to do that is to pool your efforts together with other authors doing the same thing. Together you can double the strength of your marketing platform and gain the twice the reach.

- **Bloggers/Vloggers** – Bloggers who write about a similar topic or genre also share considerable face time with your audience; in fact, many readers are first exposed to new books and authors through bloggers' recommendations. Bloggers often have open dialogue with their followers and give advice and recommendations that are trusted and credible. Seek to develop relationships with bloggers in your genre and topic by commenting on their posts, sending them review copies of your book (ask if they want them, first), sharing their links on Twitter and Facebook, offering to write guest posts on a specific theme, and brainstorming with them for cross-promotional activities. Vloggers, or video bloggers, are becoming more and more popular as well. Seek out a popular vlogger as well for your team, especially if you are YouTube challenged.

- **Publishers** – If you have a publisher or an experienced publishing consultant, these are your best industry insiders. He or she should have a good record of accomplishment in producing successful books in your genre, and should be able to provide you with tips and insights to help you get your book on bookshelves and in front of readers. Use their list of books published and the readers' reviews for an idea of the quality they can offer. It will not be perfect—no one is—but these materials should provide a general sense of the publisher's commitment to excellence. If you have a publisher, keep him or her in the loop and aware of all your marketing and publicity efforts. This helps your publisher know to keep your book stocked and where it needs to be available. Your publisher can also give you feedback on best publishing practices. With a publishing consultant, you'll want to discuss your plans and arrange for the appropriate resources to be available.

These are the primary members of your super-group, but don't be afraid to think outside the box while perusing for them. Every book and genre or topic has special needs that require different people's expertise and skills; aligning yourself with the people who can help you best learn the ins and outs of the publishing world will go a long way in helping you engage your audience and, in turn, sell more books!

How do you even get started contacting these people, you ask? Remember that, just as with your audience, you need to *provide value* before you ask for anything in return from your super-group. You are looking to cultivate *relationships*, not just take what you can get. A few key things to remember as you select your team members:

- Be sincerely interested in the other person

- Find ways to help *them* meet *their* goals

- Be willing and able to promote and/or endorse them to others

- Take time to check in and see how they are doing without looking for something in return—relationships are a series of *meaningful* interactions.

Above all, treat these individuals as you would want to be treated. If you are truly interested, considerate, and helpful, they will reciprocate in some way.

BUSINESS PLAN ELEMENTS

Budget First

After you've found the experts and mentors to make up your super-group and have begun following them on social media, it's now time to evaluate your *budget*. Your budget is the most vital aspect of any business plan, and it should include some hard numbers—on paper—that will help you determine the best options for you both in solidifying your publishing strategy and in promoting and marketing the book after publication.

Some questions to consider are:

1. What publishing options are available for writers today?

2. Which publishing option can I realistically afford (and how much money do I need to raise or save up)?

3. How many books do I want on-hand for local marketing efforts?

4. What services does my publisher (if you already have one) offer?

5. How much of my funds can I devote monthly to marketing and promoting my book?

Create a table documenting every item you need to budget for, regardless of your chosen publishing method. Include book marketing materials (posters, bookmarks, postcards, advertisements, etc.), book printing fees, publicist fees, professional headshots, and website design, plus anything else pertinent to your method of publishing.

Make sure to include printing fees, if you are self-publishing, because you will want to ensure that you have a sufficient number of books available for promotions, sending review copies, and submitting copies to bookstores for evaluation and representation. Research book vendors and ask for a quote to get an idea of how much it will cost to print the number of books you want on your first printing. Book printing can cost anywhere from $5-$15 per book, depending on your final page count and whether it's a paperback or hardcover.

If you are publishing though traditional presses, you'll need to consider the above in light of any advances you may receive, as outlined in your publishing contract.

You don't pay for printing fees yourself, of course, but it's negotiated in your contract how much advance you receive based on how much it will cost the publisher to print for you. Discuss what is included in the advance, if you have one, with your agent or publishing consultant, and budget your responsibilities and needs accordingly.

I've included a sample budget sheet with reference pricing for you below. Keep in mind that these numbers are about mid-range.

Sample Book Marketing Budget

Book marketing material - (Posters, postcards, information sheet, bookmarks, etc. Print no more than 50 of each to start, but I suggest 25)	$700
Simple website design - (You can also DIY using wix.com and still have a professional look)	$500- $1,100
Monthly marketing budget for ads & services - (This budget includes placed ads on professional websites and in magazines. Never spend this much on Facebook or any similar site. $50-$100 per month is enough.)	$1,000
Book printing fees for events - ($5x200 books)	$1,000
Professional photography for web and print use	$250

Make sure you select a company or contractor based on how they fit into your budget and on their skill set. Always look at the body of their work—one or two good book covers, for instance, does not mean they will do the same quality work on yours, whereas five or more shows a consistency that you want.

Time to Strategize

You now have your super-group and your overall budget for the project. Now it's time to solidify your *publishing strategy*.

A word to authors desiring a publishing contract: Whether you have decided to use a self-publishing press or traditional one, you must come into your talks with agents and publishers with the mindset of an authorpreneur (aka. a publishing professional) as you both discuss your publishing strategy. This does not mean that you need to attend college business courses or spend extra money on learning the publishing business inside and out. What it does mean is that you must understand what your publisher will and won't do for you, and what you in turn will need to do for yourself. An authorpreneur, at his or her roots, doesn't mind being in control—but also knows when to follow procedure and a publisher's standards.

A word to self-publishers: I understand that you are eager to get your work published. As an individual authorpreneur, however, you cannot compete with the publishing cycles of the larger firms. Your publishing strategy should focus on taking extra time to complete and perfect your publication, because you do not have the same resources available as authors going with a press, and you need that time to ensure your book is up to par.

So, what exactly *is* a publishing strategy? It's a general

timeline used to determine release dates, review requests, and organize promotional events and the like. All publishing professionals have one—it helps them to simplify deadlines and gives them a tangible way to gauge their efforts and progress. A general timeline will also allow you to develop and maintain a standard marketing schedule so you can flow with the general publishing rhythm, ensuring sufficient time to request book reviews, seek endorsements from reputable authors, and create enough "hype" about your book before its release date so you have an awaiting audience, rather than trying to build one from scratch after your book has already been released.

I cannot emphasize enough the importance of building time into your publishing schedule for getting reviews for your book *before* it's available on shelves. Book bloggers and reviewers, as discussed earlier, have a tremendous impact on your overall reputation and can help you gain credibility as an author even before your book releases. *Make getting reviews a priority in your publishing timeline!* Try to secure an agreement to review from blog reviewers, preferably those with a following of 500 or with readers who are actively posting and participating in the conversation. It's also never a waste of time to make sure you send a book with a letter of introduction and a sell sheet to reviewers like *Publisher's Weekly*, *Midwest Book Reviews*, *Library Journal*, and *Kirkus Reviews*. Pick your top 10 big name reviewers, plus another 10–20 reviewers with a good following. Only pay for reviews if you must, or if you see that they are highly influential in your target market. See some reviewer options in Appendix A.

Take a look at the suggested timeline I've included; it was designed from market data to maximize the likelihood that your books will be viewed by a larger number of established bloggers and reviewers, which will in turn increase sales. Fill in the "Book Releases" column first and work backwards—if you're running out of time to do everything, you probably need to release your book later than you originally thought.

Note that the timeline below works best for self-publishers, but you can adapt it for working with a publishing house as well—just fill in the dates that your publisher gives you for an accurate outline of how your book's development is progressing.

Suggested Publishing Timeline

Production Starts By:	Production Completed By:	Review Copies Sent:	Book Releases:
December	May	June/July	September
January	June	July	October
June	November	December/January	March
July	December	January	April

Send Post-Publication Reviews in Feb/Mar & Aug/Sept Decision Time

Now that you have all of your factors in place (your network/super-group, your overall budget, and your publishing strategy/timeline), it's time to complete, review, and make any tweaks necessary to your business plan.

1. **Revisit your budget and publishing choice.** In light of the publishing strategy you just completed, is your budget still feasible? Are you going to need more money for promotions or review copies than you originally thought? Are there additional options you may need to consider?

2. **Choose your prospective publishing team (agent, publicist, publisher, etc.).** You've probably been researching potential agents and press to work with. Now's the time to choose one and make contact. (Agents take a while to respond to queries, but you should definitely send your queries out ASAP now that you've completed your manuscript and solidified your ideal publishing strategy.) As an authorpreneur, you will want a publishing team that you feel comfortable working with, whether based on experience, personal interests, a colleague/client relationship, or compatible personalities. Even though it may take time to get them on board, or to find exactly the right agent or publisher, it's time to start stirring those waters and getting your book in front of the publishing professionals.

3. **Select your contractors.** If you're going traditional, this doesn't apply to you: your publisher will take care of this, as they already have contractors they regularly deal with. If, however, you're self-publishing, you'll need to select contractors who can print and deliver your books to you with the right look and feel that you want. Do some research on contractors, pricing, amount of books per batch, and decide which one you want to go with. (Make sure this is in your budget too!) Unless you are hiring a self-publishing company, you will need the following:

   a. **Editor** – This comes first because it's imperative to have a quality, well-edited product!

   b. **Book Cover Designer** – Also very important. Many self-published books have a "look." Find a professional within your budget who can create a high-impact cover to grab your readers' attention. Make sure they have at least ten examples of consistent, high-quality work under their belt. Leave the newbies to professional publishers who can guide them. Don't be a guinea pig!

c. **Interior Layout Designer** – This can but does not have to be your book cover designer as well.

d. **Bowker ISBN** – This is not a contractor, but it is required for each format you publish your book in. If you plan to do more than one book, buy the 10-pack ($250) at a minimum; it's more cost-effective than getting just one ($125)! Go to MyIdentifers. com to order your ISBN.

Executive Summary

Now that you have an idea of your plans, you will need to summarize it into an *executive summary*. This summary will go at the beginning of your plan, but since we had so many decisions to make, we are doing it last. Write out your publishing strategy as simply as you can. How will your book be published and by whom? When will your book be released? What steps are you taking to market it and get advance reviews? And finally, what is your budget and what will it be used for?

Congratulations: you've just created a business plan for your book! Now you really are on your way to becoming an authorpreneur!

But…the work isn't over yet.

Now we need to start contacting and reaching out to your readers.

STEP 3

CREATE YOUR AUTHOR PLATFORM

SOME AUTHORS SIMPLY give their book to family and friends and plan on that being the extent of their marketing efforts. Then, as one author said to me recently, the author "spend(s) hours on internet message boards complaining about how they have no sales and how it's impossible for the little guy to succeed." Don't be that author!

Most authors want to share their book and message with the masses. In order to do that, you have to identify your readers. In order to identify and reach those readers, you'll need a plan of action—*a marketing plan.* Without an effective one, you'll end up wasting a lot of time, money, and effort in a frenzied, unorganized attempt to sell books.

To help prevent yourself from floundering in the marketing chaos that seems to be permeating the publishing business today, follow the steps outlined in this chapter to create a book-marketing plan that will help you launch your publication with a much greater chance of success and a lesser chance of frustration.

What Is A Book Marketing Plan?

Before you begin planning how to get somewhere, you should first know where you're trying to go. A marketing plan spells out the actions needed to achieve your promotional goals. So let's start there: goals.

You may have lofty dreams and aspirations about your book getting on the bestseller's list or in Oprah's book club—and I'm not suggesting you give up on those dreams—but it's time to think about setting a *realistic, specific, and achievable goal*.

- **How many books do you want to sell in the first year?** Depending on your network size, 500 is generally just high enough to be a worthy goal but low enough to be attainable.

- **How much money do you want to make off the book in the first six months?** This number should be based on how may books you can afford to buy and re-sell, self-published or not. Any bookstore or wholesaler used can take longer to turn over revenue generated. Selling the books yourself ensures you can see the immediate return, which is highly motivating!

- **Can you make that much, or are you dreaming too big?** Everybody wants to be an overnight success, but for every one author who is, there are hundreds more who made their success the old-fashioned way: hard work and patience. Like, years of it.

It's fine to set the bar high; just make sure that your goals are *realistic, specific, and achievable.*

Write it out. Put it up on your computer desktop. Pin it to your refrigerator. Remind yourself of where you're trying to go. Once you know what goal you're shooting for and where you're headed, you can create a plan to get yourself there.

A marketing plan encompasses all aspects of the life of your book, so it's best to start with the basics.

Get Started Early: Research The Book Market

Before you even type the first sentence of your book, you can begin developing your market plan by conducting market research. You did some of this in Step 1, familiarizing yourself with the condition of the market and planning your approach. You can always refine your research at any stage of the publishing process, whether you're still writing your manuscript, are waiting to hear back from an agent, or are in talks with your publisher. There's always more to learn!

Check out the types of books that are currently selling and visit bookstores frequently to see how your specific genre or niche is currently doing or changing. Continue networking with your super-group and their audiences to gain knowledge and advice on how to refine your promotional techniques (or your approach for your next book!).

If you've already written your book, don't worry: it's never too late to research and define your book from a marketing perspective.

Five Essential Elements For Your Marketing Plan

You need to make sure you have made the following basic decisions about your book, regardless of which stage of writing or publishing you are in.

1. **First, decide on your target audience**. Go back to the original demographic you created for your beta-readers. The characteristics you were looking for then are probably similar to the ones you're looking for now, or, on the other hand, very different because you realized based on their feedback that you had targeted the wrong group of readers. Either way, use this as your starting point.

   Be *very* specific! There may be multiple groups of people that would be interested in your book, but it's best to narrow your focus from the start of your marketing efforts so you have a clear target audience.

Consider characteristics like age, gender, career, income, location, and educational background. Clarifying your targeted audience, like you did with your first beta-readers, will help you find your niche and make marketing much easier and more effective later down the line. You can then search out the best means of reaching them and begin your marketing endeavors with a clear starting point.

2. **Next, study the competition**. You did this in Step 1 as well, and may have several competing authors in your supergroup, but again, it's always good to make research continuous. The book market is *huge* and, thus, highly competitive. You can use this to your advantage, however.

   Find out what kinds of books are selling the best. Scrutinize your competitor's strengths and weaknesses, and how you can do better in that area. Record the selling price of other books based on subject, binding type, and page count.

3. **Now find out how to reach your target audience**. Go back to your readers from element one. Does your audience listen to a particular radio station, attend particular events, read a certain magazine or blog,

or have a direct connection to a particular region or city? Are there cultural ties that may influence their career choices, location, or religion? Do members of your targeted audience represent a higher percentage of the demographic in certain cities?

For example: if you are targeting young adults, you could research the location of the largest high schools in the United States. Or, if your YA novel has Roman Catholic overtones to it, you would want to narrow your search to Catholic schools in the same regions.

4. **Next, develop a statement to position your book within your targeted audience**. This statement should highlight your book's unique selling position (i.e. what separates your book from the rest of the competition). If you're not sure exactly how to answer that, consider this scenario: A reader is browsing a shelf of books and finds the opportunity to ask you directly, "Why should I buy *your* book?" What would you say? What makes your book—or your experience as its author—different from everyone else's? What special background or experience do you have as the author that will drive the audience's interest?

5. **Finally, tighten up that marketing budget**. We've already discussed this in the previous chapter, but it's a major issue that should constantly be analyzed and tweaked. How much can you realistically spend on marketing this year? Over the next two years? What type of media are you going to use? What kind of campaigns and advertisements are you going to develop? Some marketing efforts are, of course, extremely affordable, while others are outrageously expensive. Your budget will ultimately affect which promotional activities you can afford, but remember: a more expensive promotional product or strategy does not necessarily produce the best results. Do what works for your audience and your personality.

YOUR AUTHOR PLATFORM

Now that you've developed the basic goals and targeted your audience for your marketing campaign, it's time to put it to work.

The marketing plan is the broad overview of what your goals are and how to get there. Your *author platform* is how you apply it and start getting the results you want. The platform is your central hub, the outlet(s) that you use to connect with your readers and develop your online and offline presence in the publishing world.

There are dozens of tools you can use to develop your author platform, and it seems there are always more and more outlets being designed each week.

Here are a few essential tools you need to utilize in order to get started well.

Your Author Website

If you do not already have something set up, you need to get a website going, including an awesome profile and list of works. It can be as simple as a single page or as elaborate as a full-scale flash site with a blog, discussion forum, and other fun features. Every author is different and interacts with their readers differently. However you choose to design it, you should always have this basic information easily accessible on your site:

1. Your name (or pen name, if you are using a pseudonym)

2. Your basic biography

3. Book title, ISBN, summary, and planned release date

4. Instructions for purchasing (or which bookstores have it)

Once you have these basics in place, you can spruce it up with other features that enhance the reader's experience when visiting your site. Some ideas include:

- Using a newsletter sign-up form to collect your fans' information

- Creating an engaging blog

- Soliciting feedback on works-in-progress or free e-stories and asking questions of your readers related to your story

- Creating and maintaining discussion through a forum

- Adding a digital press kit (see below)

Digital Press Kit

A book's sales are often only as good as its publicity. One of the best first steps you can take to get the attention of bloggers and the media is to create a comprehensive and catchy digital press kit that is easily downloadable. *The goal of an online press kit is to provide a quick and simple way for the media and other important influencers to find out everything they need to know about you and your book(s) in one place.* It also helps your potential readers to learn more about you and see your credentials and accomplishments at a quick glance.

The content of the press kit varies from person to person, but here are my suggestions:

1. **Book info** – Include a succinct but detailed summary of your book (write it more like a news reporter and less like a salesperson).

2. **Image of the cover** – Include both a high and low resolution version for ease of use online.

3. **Author bio** – Who are you? Introduce yourself in at least three sentences.

4. **Contact info** – Include an up-to-date email address (and make sure to check it often!), as well as a phone and/or fax number, if you're comfortable with that.

5. **Anticipated media Q&A** – Think up questions a journalist might ask you for an interview, like, "What motivated you to write this book? What about this genre appeals to you? What inspired the title? Are you currently working on any new projects?" Write the answers down as if you were answering them in a live interview.

6. **Facts and figures** – Include any interesting tidbits about writing your book, such as, "It took me seven years to write the book, and I did it all in the loft of the barn on my alpaca farm," or "I wrote the entire draft freehand."

7. **Book reviews** – When you get them, display positive reviews or endorsements, starting with the ones from the most influential people.

8. **Accolades** – Show off any awards or media attention you as an author have been given or that your book has received.

9. **Book excerpts** – Present a chapter or partial chapter to intrigue fans and media members.

Social Media

The writing life is no longer cloistered and private. You've got to learn how to participate and interact with the larger conversation happening online. You do that by setting up the social media accounts that will help you maximize your platform's reach. You'll learn more about how to utilize my tools of choice effectively in the next step, but here's a basic definition of the tools many authors have success using so you can begin thinking about which ones you would like to try out.

Twitter—allows you to let the world know in 140 characters or less how awesome you and your book are. Also helps you to establish your reputation as an expert, funny guy, cultural guru, or whatever, because of the ease of communication with like-minded "tweeters" and discussion hopping.

Facebook—one of the most widely-used tools in marketing today. Allows for better information and campaign control; heavily image-based.

Goodreads—owned by Amazon, this is a leading social network for book lovers, and one of the fastest-growing communities on the Web with 3.3 million users. This site allows you to create an author page with bio, list of published books, and blog sync for free, plus bucket-loads of other features.

BookLikes—similar to Goodreads, BookLikes helps people share their reading life and discover new books. It's a blog platform designed for book lovers. What's nifty is that it does allow you to import your Goodreads data, so you are not starting over and can just add it to your list.

LibraryThing—claims to be the world's largest book club, with over 19 million books catalogued and nearly 300,000 members. Self-publishers can enroll their books in the Early-Reviewer Program to help create buzz amongst readers who receive advance copies.

Amazon Author Central—a handy place for customers to learn about you and your books. Provides essential information for readers including your biography, author photo, and blog sync.

Bookbuzzr/Freado—one of the most comprehensive online book-marketing technologies out there. Gives readers an engaging preview of your book with pages that really flip, and signs viewers up for giveaways of your book.

LinkedIn—online community for business professionals. Can help establish you as an expert with LinkedIn Answers, and offers a personal profile page to display your resume, skills, and endorsements from colleagues.

SlideShare—enables authors to easily upload and share PowerPoint presentations, PDFs, videos, and webinars online. Using SlideShare is a great opportunity to display your professional and academic understanding of a subject and leverage your influence as an expert in your field.

Pinterest—Pinterest is a site that allows users to "pin" images found on the web to virtual pinboards. There is minimal text involved because it is a visual site.

Spredd.It—a service built around making the delivery of "quotable tweets" to anywhere around the web easy with useful tools, such as real-time statistics.

Book Trailer

While not a requirement, having a book trailer that features you and your book, or a recorded interview of you, can help create buzz and encourage potential readers to purchase a copy of your book when it releases. Personally I believe that, *when executed properly, a book trailer can be the sharpest tool in your media kit*, because it's an attention grabber and can really help boost your self-published title's reputation as a legitimate, professional work. A book trailer's effectiveness is not in posting it to YouTube and watching the views roll in! Premiere the video at your book launch, like my author David Jackson did with his book video for *The Man Behind the Music*, prepared by *Trailer to the Stars!* Take your trailer to other blogs, add it to your Amazon page, and find dedicated book trailer websites like ChristianBookVideos.com that you can post your trailer to. You should also **ask** reviewers to include the trailer with their reviews or interviews. A book trailer is a tool to be *used*; do not set it aside and allow the dust to settle!

Did you see the catch? An effective book trailer is all about these three words: "when executed properly." A great book trailer can really set you apart from the competition, but a sloppy one can make you out as amateurish. You also will not feel comfortable drawing attention to it, which makes it useless.

To help prevent that detrimental result from happening, honestly assess your abilities by asking yourself these three questions:

1. **Am I *skilled* enough to create a book trailer?** Some people just don't have the artistic skills to make a professional book trailer. You know who you are...wherever your deficiency lies, whether it's not

knowing your way around a computer, not possessing strong visual creativity, or struggling with new technologies and programs, it's okay to acknowledge that your forte lies in other areas (like writing a book!) and leave your book trailer up to the professional artists. Believe me, you'll thank yourself later.

2. **Do I have the *time* to create a book trailer?** Even if you have the skills, odds are you're already up to your eyeballs in writing, managing your author platform, soliciting reviews, and querying agents and publishers. Making a *good* book trailer takes serious time and focus—that's why there are freelancers and even entire companies who are dedicated to nothing but creating trailers for authors. If you don't have enough time or focus to allocate to the project, it's wiser to hire someone who does.

3. **What is my book trailer *budget*?** Whether hiring out or designing your own, creating a book trailer has its costs. From purchasing stock photos to visual equipment to editing software, or hiring actors or voice-over artists or a scriptwriter, you could easily be looking at an investment

of several hundred dollars. Like everything stated previously, *do your research!* There is a compiled list of resources in the appendices at the end of this book that can get you started, and you can also utilize the freelance websites I mentioned in Step 1: MediaBistro, Elance, Guru, and Craigslist. Fiverr.com is another option I have heard authors having success with. (We at Ellechor Media use producer Misty Taggart from *Trailer to the Stars!*, and we highly recommend her team's work! If you decide to use her service, **mention this book for a discount**.)

Soliciting Endorsements

The most important goal for establishing your author platform is to develop an easy-to-access author personality that readers can trust and believe in. Your credibility as an author starts with the steps above, but it is truly enhanced with endorsements from top industry influencers and notable figures in your field or genre.

Endorsements lend credibility to you and your work, pump up your publicity, influence booksellers to purchase orders for bookstores, and grab the attention of potential readers who will be more likely to buy the book off the shelf or e-store when they see the celebrity name that is recommending the book to them. Getting these endorsements is critical to establishing your credibility, and I always advise authors to start soliciting them as soon as possible.

How do you go about obtaining them? Admittedly, it requires a bit of work, but the benefits far outweigh the initial difficulties you may run into.

1. **The first step is to evaluate the super-group you established in Step 2.** Consider experts in your field if you write non-fiction and writers of similar genre if you write fiction. Are there any potential endorsers amongst them whose recommendation you would really love to have? Any who you can contact directly or have a mutual colleague contact for you?

2. **Determine if they're appropriate for your book's subject or genre.** I find the most effective endorsements are from other authors or field experts who have written a book, particularly bestselling ones. Look specifically at the bestselling authors in your super-group, and see if you can contact them directly, find a mutual colleague to do so for you, or contact them through their publisher or agent. Celebrity endorsements, even from ones who haven't written a book, are also helpful as well, if the celebrity is known to have an interest

in the subject matter, for instance. Well-known business leaders are great for business books or topics focusing on leadership, marketing, entrepreneurship, communication, and the like. Remember to consider the different audiences of your book and work toward collecting endorsements from people who they would recognize and listen to.

3. **Request the endorsements via cover letter.** Prepare a clean copy of your manuscript or a full Advanced Reader Copy (ARC) along with your cover letter. You can include a sample endorsement or two in the letter and encourage the endorser to use or modify one of them, or, on the other hand, write one of their own. Pre-written endorsements not only improve your chances of receiving a recommendation from your selected endorser, but they also help emphasize the selling points you're hoping to publicize. Keep the samples short and sweet—just a couple sentences is an ideal length for capturing readers' and buyers' attention.

4. **Utilize the endorsements you receive.** In order for endorsements to bring you the most benefit, you have to place them

strategically into your marketing plan to attract readers who may be influenced by that particular expert or celebrity you solicited the endorsement from. Good places to include the endorsements are:

> › On the sidebar or key pages of your website, along with pertinent information about the endorser

> › On the back cover or interior of your book (check with your publisher)

> › In your digital press kit and on your sell sheet

> › On your social media pages (a recommendation via Facebook or a few "tweets" on Twitter to let your fans know a certain celebrity or major industry expert has just endorsed you is a huge selling point)

KEEPING IT GOING

All this may seem a little overwhelming at first, but once you try it, bit by bit, you'll find yourself becoming more market-savvy and knowledgeable of how to reach your readers. Remember that the marketing is not only about turning over sales; it's about projecting your entire brand—your personality, experience, and author voice—to consumers. Creating a high-profile website and/or blog, soliciting reviews and endorsements, staying active on social media, and promoting your book through trailers and visual images are all ways to help you build your author platform and gain credibility as a true professional—an authorpreneur.

Here are some additional last thoughts on the mindset it's imperative to have as you create and continue utilizing your marketing plan.

1. **Quality first**. The fastest way to failure is mediocrity and blending in with the crowd. Your long-term success depends on satisfied customers who spread the word about your book and encourage others to purchase from you. If your book and overall brand aren't top quality, you won't get their referrals or attract the right attention from influencers. Remember to continually highlight what qualities make you different from your competition.

2. **Build relationships**. Create real relationships with your super-group, publishing team, and potential readers. Ask yourself periodically what you are doing to get noticed or to connect with your fans. Answer their questions, solve their problems, and help them when they're stuck. Offer an opinion and see what theirs are. Your network and readers want to know there's a real person in there somewhere;

show them who you are, and care about who *they* are.

3. **Stay committed**. If your marketing efforts are going to take hold, then you need to commit to sticking with it through thick and thin. Don't give up in the early stages when you don't have a whole lot to go on yet, and also don't be afraid to revisit your plan and make changes or reinvent aspects that aren't working.

4. **Be consistent**. Marketing for the author is much like breathing—it's the life of your small business (you!), and should be a regular part of your daily activities. Make sure to stay visible on your social media outlets and blog, if you have one, and create a consistent presence where people can see you. Just a few minutes a day is all it takes, and it will go a long way to help keep you from disappearing in the crowd.

5. **Make it easy**. If the purchasing process, marketing materials, or any other part of your book promotion or author platform is too complicated to access, your customers will become confused and frustrated, and probably leave. Confused or frustrated customers simply don't buy. Make sure to streamline the purchasing process with as

few steps as possible to make it easy for readers to purchase your work.

6. **Automate**. We live in a fast-track society; embrace automation tools like email auto-responders, shopping carts, social media responders, landing pages, customer management software, and the like. A few nifty tools include:

   a. *TweetDeck* by Twitter, an app that allows you to schedule your posts across multiple social media platforms

   b. *Buffer*, a free app that allows you to set the specific time(s) of day for your posts, or you can let it decide when your fans are most active. You can create your buffer collection of posts by writing them out or by using their app to "buffer" the sites and posts you come across. It also allows you to post to LinkedIn company pages. (Full disclosure: I use this application.)

   c. *HootSuite*, which is similar to TweetDeck, but has more robust features available for a price

   d. *SproutSocial*, a paid service that adds what TweetDeck and Hootsuite offer, plus throws in the ability to view statistics on your posts, the likes you have received over a specific period, and allows you to compare your social media page to other users. (Additional disclosure: I loved this app but did not want to pay for it.)

e. *Facebook,* which has become very anti-external automation tools, but if you have the time, you can set up your posts on Facebook using their (not so fun) post-scheduling option. It will decrease your reach if you use an external posting application, but if the majority of your fans are not on Facebook, then it does not matter. Of course, you can also get around it by paying for your posts to be promoted.

7. **Rinse and repeat**. Research suggests that prospects need to encounter a product between seven and twelve times before they are ready to purchase! So, put your book in front of your target market over and over again. Be careful not to spam followers, however! Look for *authentic* ways to deliver your message and engage with your readers without sounding like a commercial or clogging up their social media

feeds and inboxes with "Buy Me!" links (more on this in Step 4).

8. **Track results.** It's essential to your overall marketing survival that you have a clear understanding of what is working and what isn't. You don't want to keep wasting time and energy on things that aren't worth the effort. Use link-tracking software to track your Return On Investment (ROI) so you can be prepared to adjust your plan if necessary.

9. **Have patience.** The fruits of your marketing labors won't show up overnight. You have to plant your marketing seeds and tend them *regularly* before your marketing "garden" blooms. And don't worry, it will!

STEP 4

ENGAGE YOUR AUDIENCE

WE'VE TALKED A lot about building your platform and creating an effective marketing plan, as well as the tools you can use to stay in touch with your readers and audience.

"But these are just the tools," you may be saying. "What do I actually *say* to them?!"

That's what this chapter is all about: how to engage your audience with real, authentic conversation and develop a thriving, fun community on your author platform.

All the aspects discussed in this chapter are things you will need to do continually, not just a one-time action like setting up a website or signing up for a Twitter account. Your readers are real people and are constantly watching your platform for glimpses of you or your next big project. Make sure to interact with them regularly!

THE RIGHT SELF-PROMOTION MINDSET

Self-promotion is the strongest way to build your credibility as an author. But there's a right way and a wrong way to go about it.

If you do too much of it, you come across as a spammer and egotistical, which annoys your readers and often makes them become someone else's readers. On the other hand, doing little to no self-promotion isn't effective either because your book never gets in front of your potential readers or gets their attention in the first place.

I'll give you the secret right here: the most effective way to self-promote without being labeled a spammer or egotist is to *develop a natural, friendly Web presence that engages readers' interests and shows off your work...without sounding like a commercial.*

These days there is an art to writing and an art to self-promotion. If you view your writing as art and your self-promotion efforts as the furthest thing from art, then your chance of developing a successful 21st-century writing career is going to remain slim to none. From the moment you start putting words to the page, it's never too early to start thinking about how you're going to share those words with the public. Once you begin seeing your writing and promotional efforts as equally artful, something wonderful begins to happen: you find readers.

Books, as you know, are not written overnight—they're developed one day at a time—and it's the same way with your author platform, which comprises all the ways you make yourself visible to your readers. All the work you've done so far in setting up social media accounts, budgeting, building a website, and putting plans in place to develop your author platform may have seemed overwhelming at first. But, if you consistently take small steps to put yourself out there authentically, before you know it you will have built a strong, sturdy foundation for your work.

So, if you're the kind of writer who prefers being read to being unknown (who doesn't?), take a look through these 5 simple but major ways to start launching your platform into action and engaging your readers through a fun, professional community. Think of each small step as a giant leap toward finding and drawing in readers—and a fun, rewarding opportunity to share your hard-wrought words with others, as you've wanted to do for so long.

1. **Listen & Learn**

    a. **Find your keepers**. You may have more than one audience, and that's great if you do—you'll have a farther reach—but which one do you want to connect with *immediately*? You'll spread yourself too thin if you try to engage all your audiences at once, because they may all require different communication and levels of involvement. Pick one, and start with them (you can branch out later); these are your "keepers," the ones you will speak to through your blog and social media outlets, and who will be your primary target group during your promotional efforts.

b. **Start surveillance**. Google Alerts can help you become practically omnipresent in only a few clicks. Take five minutes to set up alerts to notify you when your name, articles, blog posts, book title, Twitter handle, site URL, and/or your specialty topics pop up online. When you receive an alert that someone promoted your name, shared your idea, or supported your work in some other way, stick your virtual hand out and say, "Hey, thanks! I appreciate that!"

c. **Poll for solutions**. Ask questions. You'll get answers. If you're wondering which hosting service or stock photo site to use, or if people seem to be having the same server problems you are, try posting a question about it on Facebook, LinkedIn, or Twitter. I do this often and love receiving answers from other authors and experts. After you get your answer, share it right back with others!

d. **Show respect**. Whether on social networks or in person, "follow" and "friend" folks in your industry or genre whom you admire. Steer clear of anyone shifty, clingy, or shilling stuff all the time (a good rule of thumb is to avoid promoting or forwarding the cause of anyone online that you wouldn't in real life, and vice versa). It takes time to get to know people, but it's worth it when your reputation is on the line. Be polite and courteous to everyone you meet, and seek to avoid confrontational discussions or brow-beating others who disagree with you on something. We're all in this publishing thing together.

e. **Study the competition**. Yes, we've talked about this quite a bit, but as I've said before, it's a vital habit for authorpreneurs to get into. Jump on a search engine periodically and type in the keywords that describe what you write about. See who pops up on your radar. Don't be afraid of the competition; study your competitors closely (without becoming a stalker, of course). What are they doing better than you? Add what you learn or a technique you'd like to try to your marketing to-do list.

2. Create Context

a. **Introduce yourself well**. Take a few minutes or more to write a brief bio you can use wherever your name appears online—it can be different than the one in your press kit (briefer and more succinct, or funnier/drier, etc.). Include your URL, relevant professional credentials, recent publications (both online and off), significant self-published work, professional partnerships and memberships, etc.—but keep it to no more than three sentences long.

b. **Show yourself in action**. I bet you have a whole bunch of photos of yourself out and about doing what you do. If some are shots of you writing, great…but, it is even better if you have some decent-quality photos of you speaking, teaching a workshop, signing books at an event, and the like. Collect them and use them to accompany your posts or articles online.

c. **Post ads and affiliate links**. You have to have or make money to invest money in your platform, so why not make the most of the resources and tools you already like? You won't get rich from affiliate revenue, but it can add up over the course of a year and cover some of your ongoing platform expenses. Though you should be very selective about which products and companies you choose to represent on your site, it only takes minutes to post an ad or affiliate link on your website or blog once you've done so.

d. **Hold an event**. Create a promotional event or giveaway that has a time limit (like a week-long or 30-day event) and a specific step that needs to be completed. Create whatever type of event is appropriate for what you write—perhaps a quiz or prizes for book reviewers within a certain period. Create an environment that draws your tribe in, helps people interact with each other, and converts folks into loyal fans who will keep coming back for more (free stuff helps). Dream something up.

e. **Get graded**. HubSpot has a free tool at Marketing.Grader.com that gauges the effectiveness of your website, blog, Facebook page, and Twitter account, among other things. Each grader takes less than five minutes to run. Check your platform on one periodically and add its suggestions to your marketing to-do list. I personally have started grading my websites; the first grade we got was passable but eye-opening.

3. **Contribute Content**

a. **Give it away**. Spread the word across your social networks for your audience to come and get whatever you can give away for free, whether it's an article, eBook, or blog post series. If you already wrote an article or short story you don't plan to sell, why not give it away? People love free, and they'll thank you for it often by becoming loyal fans who promote you to others.

b. **Brainstorm 20 ideas**. If you don't constantly ask yourself what new ideas you have, half of them will get away from you. Then you'll have to read your idea on someone's blog or in a magazine or newspaper beside someone else's byline. So, get into the habit of writing down your creative ideas, both for new stories and books and for your platform and blog as well, in an idea journal. Drain your brain into it for five minutes at a time, and do it again in a few weeks to stay fresh.

c. **Put your best forward**. Make sure people who are just discovering your offerings can go straight to some of your online writing that represents your creativity at its best. Even if it's not connected to your current release, this great content is in danger of getting buried under your latest efforts, when instead it can be a highlighted feature of your site that shows people that you've been a professional in the making for a long time. Create a way to send fans and followers straight to your best posts, either with a "Best

Of" page, a "See Also" link at the end of your blog posts, or by utilizing widgets most blogging platforms have which will do the rounding up for you based on the number of hits each post has.

d. **Recycle**. Take a few minutes to pitch content that you've already written to make room for a new outlet. Can you find a blog, forum, or association newsletter that might be interested in your topic? What about a content curator like Constant-Content.com? This site requires unique material, but if you don't have time, you can always rework your old articles to get them updated and fresh before submitting. It's also a good idea to start with a site like this, and then repost from them later.

e. **Review worthy writers**. What goes around comes around, and inquiring readers like to know which books you enjoy and why. Reviewing other authors' works helps people to see that you are personable and professional by having your ear to the ground (or eye to the page), and that you're keeping abreast of the industry and watching for and supporting newcomers. Briefly review books as you read them and post your insights on your review sites like Goodreads, BookLikes, Amazon, and on your own blog. For good karma, sing the praises of your all-time favorites, too. Don't have time to write a full review? Video blogging your reviews is another option, especially if you always look good!

4. **Cultivate Community**

   a. **Prompt a response**. A prompt is a suggestive word or theme that cues an interactive response from others. It can be as simple as a photo, symbol, or word, or as complicated as a riddle or scavenger hunt. For example, when I hosted an annual book giveaway, I asked a question of my readers each day for a month, and everyone who responded was entered in a drawing. Participants loved the prompt more than the free books! Prompts are a fun way to interact with and nurture your growing online community.

   b. **Take five to interact**. Reply to comments on your blog. Thank people who download your free content. Retweet a link or give a shout out to their content on your social network. Think of three people to appreciate for any reason at all. Spend a little time with those who have gone out of their way to care about you.

c. **Make an engaging offer**. If you're working on a project and decide that you need people to get involved from the get-go, offer something—like a discount or kickback—to the first 50 people who express interest. Create excitement for those who are willing to work with you by utilizing your social media outlets and newsletters to generate buzz.

d. **Form strategic partnerships**. Who do you want on your side or as a colleague? Being friendly and helpful should have no strings attached—but true partnerships are mutually beneficial, formal agreements in which each part is hoping to gain something specific. List three likely partners and reach out to them, whether upcoming authors, bloggers, experts, or scholars.

e. **Create a quickie blogroll.** Make a list of writers and experts you admire. Search for their website or blog and add them to your blogroll so that others can discover them, too. Position your blog as an inspiring resource for others by going for quality, not quantity.

5. *Be Authentic*

a. **Be yourself.** The advice you hear all over the web that tells authors to act like brands encourages them to forget to act like regular people. Social media and discussion is made for people, not robots. The fact that you're a writer and a parent, uncle, Packers fan, or vegetarian makes you interesting. Your readers and fans want you to be personable, not an ever-plugging, one-topic broken record. Look for ways to periodically tweak your profile to make it more you as you change and evolve as a person and author over the years.

b. **Put passion into action.** No matter your passion—even if it's literary fiction, supposedly "harder to build a platform around"—take it online and put it to work. Don't assume no one cares—assume millions of people care! Start connecting with the people out there like you who love this genre or topic. Take a few minutes to write a mission statement about why you're on fire for this subject, then reread it every time you get online to help you focus your efforts and remember why you do what you do.

c. **Get together**. Make sure you tell folks about your events and signings. Let your readers know you'll be in their area for your next speaking or teaching event, and make yourself accessible to them by sharing your itinerary. Allow people to be able to contact and socialize with you at your events without making it too difficult for them to find you.

d. **Spark conversations**. Other people are just as passionate about your topic as you are. Get on Google, Twitter, and discussion forums where your topic is trending and spend a few minutes participating in a chat. Share the passion and enjoy the conversation! If no one seems to be talking about it, strike up your own conversation.

e. **Share the journey**. You have a lot going on right now, I'm sure. Surely some of it is interesting, or you have a unique perspective on a seemingly mundane topic. Update others on what's happening in your life right now. Don't keep your ups and downs a secret—people want to see you as a real human being...plus, curious fans love to be treated like insiders.

See how very few of these are actually "buy me" actions? People want to invest in *people*, so be a person and make your self-promotion tactics about being real and authentic, not a bookseller. If you can win people over so they like *you*, I guarantee they'll trust you a lot more and want to support you by buying your book and/or promoting you to others.

SOCIAL MEDIA: THE SELF-PROMOTION TOOLKIT

Social media can be overwhelming, but it doesn't have to be. If you come at it with the attitude that you're there to build a community, make new friends, and have fun (with a teeny bit of marketing on the side), you'll find that social media is a terrific way to connect with your readers and advance your career as a do-it-yourself authorpreneur. Building an effective, active social media network takes time, patience, and perseverance, but successful campaigns happen 365 days a year; you never know how your outreach will affect sales or procure consultation requests, speaking opportunities, or new business endeavors.

You are not required to participate in every social network available or spend your entire day promoting yourself! When you were setting up your platform back in Step 3, you should have picked the social media outlets that were/are most relevant to your platform and match well with your personality and comfort. A few tips to keep in mind:

- Automated tools like Buffer, HootSuite, and SproutSocial can help you post to most of your media accounts—choose only one!

- Determine beforehand what amount of time you have available each day or week, and devote that time consistently.

- High-quality, relevant posts are more important than volume.

- The key to effective social media marketing is engagement—be willing and able to interact with others, and pay it forward when it comes to sharing other people's activities and information.

- Be yourself! Authenticity is the key to drawing people in and sharing your message.

There are hundreds of resources detailing the many social media tools and services available. I'm just going to cover some details for six of the most popular and effective ones below. Remember that you *can* create profiles on all of them, but you should and need to only focus on one or two.

Twitter—Twitter: your life, right now, in 140 characters or less. It's one of the largest ongoing conversations on the web, and it's easy to jump into the "stream" whenever you feel like it. There are several tools available to help you increase the number of followers and establish yourself as an expert in your field, including:

- Recommendations that Twitter provides on your homepage. The server automatically analyzes your existing followers and the subject matter of your tweets and makes recommendations of other "tweeters" you should consider following.

- Twibes.com, which allows users to become members of an existing group of people sharing a common interest; additionally, users can also start their own group.

- Commun.it, a robust Twitter relationship management tool helps you find the most valuable members within your Twitter community and beyond it by auto-sorting your followers into "influencers," "supporters," and "engaged members." In addition, you can set up specific keyword searches, and Communi. it will find the people who have those keywords in their profile or tweet about those keywords often. It will then list those people for you based on their level of influence on Twitter.

If you want to reward your followers for interacting with you, one of the best ways is to hold a Twitter giveaway. You could give away a book or a free consultation or interview, or the winner could name a character in your next book. Check out contest-focused apps and services like Offerpop.com's "NewFollower" app, and Tweetsw.in [sic] if you have more than 500 followers already, for help choosing a random winner.

There's nothing worse than a boring tweeter. Try to vary your posts and add in some real life stuff, like what you're currently doing or an interesting idea you just had, but also include a call-to-action, links to documents, photos, or videos, and retweets of your fellow authors and experts to share new things with your followers. Make liberal use of hashtags (the # symbol), which is the Twitter system for enabling people to search for and follow tweets that include that particular keyword following the hashtag and join in the conversation—#books, for instance, or #marketing. You can also create your own hashtags that are original to you, like #titleofyourbook or #yourcharactername.

Some Twitter tools that can enhance the content of your tweets are:

- TwitDoc.com for document sharing
- TwitPic.com for photo sharing
- TwitVid.com for video sharing

Facebook—Facebook is a visual social media—while discussion should occur frequently on Facebook, pictures go a long way and are more likely to be reposted or shared amongst your followers.

To kick-start your Facebook network, it's preferable for authors to start a fan page rather than a group. While Facebook prefers you only have a fan page and your personal page, I also created a professional Facebook account to manage my company pages. It allows me to interact freely with my authors, clients, and professional friends without the clutter of my personal rants. I also can add whomever I wish to get to know—and my page is public, so anyone looking for me usually stops there!

Fan pages help you promote your personal brand, build a network, and raise visibility and public interaction with your community. They allow you to post new and existing discussions, send messages to all members via updates, analyze visitor statistics, create events, and invite fans to your upcoming events. You can also track fan demographics and viral posts, as well as your overall reach on the network. Fan pages are also much more visible to search engines, and you can create a unique URL that you can connect to your overall brand (i.e. Facebook.com/yourauthorname).

Groups, on the other hand, are designed merely for online discussion of similar interests, with limited features only allowing for discussions, chat messages to all members rather than personal messages to individuals, and participation in public video or photo exchanges. You can't view your group visitor stats, and groups are not visible to search engines. Your URL is also a jumbled mixture of random letters and numbers, which makes it very difficult to share with others unless you use a tool like bit.ly to shorten and customize it.

Goodreads—This is a great social networking site for authors and their readers. Since it connects to Facebook, you can publish your reviews and recommend your book to your entire social media network. It contains author features that allow authors to:

1. Publicize upcoming events, such as book signings and speaking engagements

2. Tap influencers and get books in the hands of fans by listing a book giveaway

3. Gather reader feedback by creating custom trivia questions and online polls

4. Interact with readers by participating in an online Q&A session

It does require you to list yourself as an author, so here are some quick steps as provided by Goodreads to getting started:

1. If you are already a Goodreads member, make sure you are signed in. If not, sign up for an account.

2. Search for and click on your published author name. The author name is listed below the title of your book in the search results. If you do not find your book in the Goodreads database of published works, you will need to become a "librarian" to add it. You can find information on that process on their website.

3. Clicking on your name takes you to your basic author profile page. This page has your name at the top and "author profile" to the right of your name. This page is part of their database of books and authors and is separate from your member profile page (which lists your bookshelves and friends).

4. Scroll down to the bottom of the page. Click "*Is this you?*" to send a request to join the Author Program. After a few days, you will receive email confirmation that Goodreads has successfully upgraded your user account to an author account. Joining the program merges your author page with your member page. The email will also contain further instructions for managing your author profile.

Amazon Author Central—At Author Central, you can share the most up-to-date information about yourself and your works with millions of readers. You can also see timely sales data for free, including sales trends over time and where in the US your books are selling. To set up your account, follow these steps:

1. Go to AuthorCentral.Amazon.com and click "*Join Now.*"

2. Enter your e-mail address and password and click "*Sign in using our secure server.*"

> If you have an Amazon.com account, sign in with the e-mail address and password you use on that account.

> If you do not have an existing Amazon account, select "*No, I am a new*

customer." You will be prompted to enter the necessary information.

3. Read the Author Central's Terms and Conditions, and then click *"Agree"* to accept them.

4. Enter the name your books are written under. A list of possible book matches appears.

5. Select any one of your books. If your book is not in the list, you can search for it by title or ISBN. The book you select must be available for purchase on the Amazon website. Selecting the book creates the account.

6. When you receive the confirmation e-mail, confirm your e-mail address and identity.

Now that you are up and running, add your biography, photos, blog feed, video, and tour events to the Author Page, your homepage on Amazon. You can also add Facebook and Twitter feeds. This site is low-maintenance and important, since the vast majority of sales are by Amazon.

LinkedIn—Of all the social media networks, LinkedIn is the most business-oriented. The vast majority of LinkedIn users are involved in business of some kind, and therefore can make great connections for authors who want to sell books in bulk to companies, speak at events, or otherwise connect with influential business leaders. Following are my top 5 ways to make the most out of your efforts on LinkedIn:

1. **Complete your profile**–LinkedIn users often use the search feature to find resources. In order to be found, your profile should be loaded with keyword-rich content. Choose a descriptive title, and be sure to fill out the "Experience" section in a way that ties it to your book and your qualifications as an authorpreneur.

2. **Feature your book**–In the "Publications" section, you can list details about books you've written or contributed to, including a synopsis of each and a link to learn more about the book.

3. **Participate in groups**–Groups on LinkedIn are typically quite active. Find one book/business-related group and use it to help you build your author platform. Post, reply, and participate in the group actively.

4. **Get recommendations**–Solicit recommendations for your book, for you as a speaker, and for your business. Recommendations are prominently displayed on your profile and add an element of credibility. Reach out

to your contacts and ask for recommendations. In return, you should plan to give some recommendations as well.

5. **Get endorsements**–LinkedIn allows people to easily click a button and "endorse" your skills and expertise. You will indicate the skills that you want to be known for by adding these when editing your profile. LinkedIn will automatically begin to ask your connections to endorse you.

Pinterest—Again, Pinterest is a site that allows users to "pin" images found on the web to virtual pinboards. There's minimal text involved because it's a visual site. Personally, I think your time would be better spent with more tried-and-true sites, but if you really connect with this medium (as one author who specifically requested more information on this did) and want to do some professional pinning, here are five ideas:

1. **Create a novel inspiration pinboard**– Tease your fans by creating a pinboard that showcases photos of people and locations that inspired your upcoming book.

2. **Create a novel comparison pinboard**– Think of the authors within your genre who write stories similar to your own. Gather their book covers, along with your

own, and put them on a pinboard. This can be your "If you like _____, you'll also like my book!" board.

3. **Create an upcoming cover art pinboard**—Fans love leaked images, so when you begin working through cover designs with your publisher (or even if you e-publish!), be sure to "leak" the images to your pinboard.

4. **Create a blog pinboard**—Some authors see success with Pinterest when they consistently pin photos from their blog posts. This requires you to (a) maintain a blog, (b) include photos with each post, and (c) properly pin those photos.

Additional tips: Create great, concise descriptions of each pin, use hashtags, keywords, and links, and be sure to pin book covers from sites on which the book can actually be purchased. Lastly, tag every book cover pin with genre, author, and title information.

KEEP UP WITH EVERYONE

One more thing to consider before we wrap up: how in the world do you keep track of all these new people you meet? How do you decide which ones are just readers and which ones are experts or potential additional members of your super-group or professional network?

Authors are constantly chasing down opportunities to share their book, speak to a crowd, serve as a resource, and engage in other platform-building activities. Nevertheless, opportunities are everywhere...and authors often get lost trying to figure out which ones to try first.

The best thing you can do for yourself is to keep track of *leads*, or people who you'd like to get to know better because you believe they may be beneficial to your overall career, whether as an adviser, mentor, friend, or because of their connections with others you're looking to connect with. Leads are *not* everyone in your social network! They are the key people, the professionals and colleagues, that it would be advantageous for you to know better.

Cultivating these relationships is crucial to your career, but they don't need to take up all your time, either. The first thing you need to do, *as soon as you meet a lead*, is to gather their contact information. Enter the info into a simple database like Microsoft Outlook or PlanPlus. Unlike spreadsheets and rolodexes, databases like these allow you to classify your contact, set up reminders, add notes, and keep track of all interactions. It might also be helpful to add the contact to your LinkedIn or Twitter network if you believe you know the person well enough to engage them online.

Make sure you categorize your leads! Not all of

them are equal in benefit to you, and each category will require a certain amount of interaction. A simple way to classify your leads is as:

1. **A Hot Lead:** These are people interested in having you speak or who want to schedule you for some event. These contacts are ready to go and need to receive frequent, personal contact in order for the relationship to develop into an event or opportunity. These contacts go to the top of your list.

2. **A Warm Lead:** These are people who have shown interest, but who have not yet decided whether they want to or can work with you. You will need to provide them with more information and interaction, and work to cultivate the relationship.

3. **A Cold Lead:** Cold leads are people with whom you have no rapport, such as those you find on the web or found out about through third-party sources. These contacts are usually managed through what is called "drip line marketing." Drip line marketing consists of things like newsletters or emails you send out to a distribution list on an infrequent basis. You may need to send an introductory email to

them and then a reminder a few months later, or add them to an informational newsletter until they opt out or say they are not interested. Setting up a drip line campaign helps you to educate potential clients who may very well turn into A or B leads if given the right amount of time.

Sorting your leads into these categories will help you better identify and manage opportunities as they come.

It takes at least six points of contact for a message to sink in—yes, *six*—yet more than 75 percent of the time, people stop pursuing leads after the first point of contact (*Good Day* 2009). Don't do this! Just because you don't receive an answer at first or get a rejection doesn't mean that you should drop that lead completely. Come up with creative ways (a drip-line campaign) to benefit *them* and establish communication, even if it's not about your book or marketing campaign at first. Don't forget to provide value first, and remember that **your leads are people**. Treat them with respect and consideration, and always show your appreciation for their time, regardless of the outcome.

THE END RESULT

Like the previous chapter, some of this may seem overwhelming to you. Don't be intimidated; engaging your audience is fun! Taking little steps each day to say hi to someone, say thank you, or to ask for their opinion on something can really go a long way in developing your brand and reputation as a nice person with a professional attitude and a great rapport with their readers. Engaging your audience with authenticity and respect will help you increase sales over time because you have established your credibility and trustworthiness as an author, rather than making your marketing all about how great your work is. Readers like friendly authors, so be friendly and have fun!

STEP 5

GET READY TO LAUNCH

WELL, YOU'RE HERE at long last. You've written your book and had it professionally edited (maybe even accepted by an agent or publisher!), developed your business and marketing plan, created the beginnings of your author platform, and have started engaging with professional leads and your target audience in a friendly way. People are starting to expect your book now and are eager to read it.

So, it's time to get the book into their hands!

Whether you chose at the beginning of this book to self-publish or have pursued a traditional publishing route, these launching tips will help you stay focused and keep your hands on your writing career instead of giving it over to others—the way an authorpreneur handles their career!

There are four things you need to do before we get that book printed and on the shelves:

1. Write a press release

2. Query for interviews

3. Request early reviews

4. Host a pre-launch event

YOUR PRESS RELEASE

You may have spent years writing your masterpiece, and you thought the hard part was over. Actually now you have, quite possibly, a harder task in front of you: getting the media's attention. Your author platform has helped you get the attention of some readers, which is great—but the real attention and sales boost is going to come from the media. The best way to do that is to write a press release that you can send them.

- Make sure the headline packs a punch. Look for news, current events, holidays, comparable movie or book titles, and attention-catching happenings that you can tie your book to.

- Be creative, but on topic. Make the release newsworthy (make a big deal about it), objective, and accurate. Try to send out new releases as you find relevant newsworthy items to connect your book to, no more than every 4-6 weeks, and only during the first six months to a year after your book's release.

- Include the most important information in the first two paragraphs and the least important at the bottom, in the inverted triangle style.

- Explain the relevance and benefit of your book to the intended audience.

- Make sure the release isn't self-centered and does not sound like a sales pitch—**it should read like a newspaper or magazine story.**

- For increased visibility online, use relevant keywords and terms that search engines will latch onto, if you're going with an online press release site. Find new offline places to send each release as well, and cultivate a professional relationship whenever possible.

- List your book's bibliographic data (ISBN, publish date, price, page count, etc.) and display the cover image.

- Be sure to include your contact information, or that of your publisher or publicist, for people who want more information or to request an interview with you.

REQUESTING INTERVIEWS

One of the best ways to add credibility, gain publicity, and engage your audience is by getting your name out there through interviews. You can do this through the blogging community, or offline mediums like magazines and newspapers. My favorite websites to search for programs to pitch to are:

- *HelpAReporter.com*–HARO is entirely free to sources and reporters, and serves as a vital social networking resource for sources, reporters, and advertisers who use the service

- *RadioGuestList.com*–Radio Guest List compiles free lists of radio and blog talk radio stations that are looking for guests, and connects them with potential sources. It also allows experts/authors and the like to promote themselves as potential guests, for a fee.

- *BlogTalkRadio.com*–TR hosts a variety of Blog Talk Radio shows and is a great resource if you want to find a show specific to your genre and topic, or if you just want to find author-centric shows and pitch to them exclusively.

If you've done your market research well, you'll be familiar with the major publications your target audience reads. If you are a business author, for instance, you will know that your readers are likely subscribed to *Forbes, Entrepreneur, Inc.*, or other similar publications. If you are a fantasy author, you will probably be familiar with *Fantasy & Science Fiction* and *Clarke's World*. Do some research using MyMediaInfo or Vocus to find the appropriate editor or contact for each publication, or you can find it on their individual websites.

The Pitch

Once you have identified the appropriate contact, develop a pitch for getting interviewed. The pitch needs to give a clear, single-sentenced hook that will establish why you'd be a good interviewee and the premise that you'd like the interviewer to focus on. The hook should answer the following questions the interviewer will have when reading your pitch:

1. Who are you, the author?

2. What value can you, the author, provide to my (the editor's) readership?

3. What sets you apart from others in your field?

For instance, your hook could be, "My name is John Smith, and I developed a five-step program for strategic management that has been adopted by twenty of the top Fortune 500 companies."

This hook should open up your cover letter to the editor or interviewer. Make sure to attach your press kit to the letter, since it provides the media with everything they need to determine whether you are a good candidate and will serve as a great starting point for them to develop their questions and angle if they decide to interview you.

The Interview Itself

1. **Develop talking points** – Most interviews will focus on a few basic points and angles, which means you can walk into almost any interview already prepared, but you will also have to be ready to shoot from the hip occasionally. Practice keeping your answer short and to the point and free of technical jargon so a broad audience can understand what you're saying without having to do any follow-up. Basic media questions include:

   › What is the title of your book?

   › What is it about?

   › Why did you decide to write it?

   › Who should read your book and why?

   › What authority do you have to write on this topic?

   › Where can people find out more about you and your book?

   Even if these questions are not asked,

they are points you will want to work into the conversation yourself. The most important pieces of information you want to convey to your audience are your book title and where it can be purchased. In fact, you will want to mention the title and its accompanying website several times throughout the interview, if possible. Repetition is key! An appearance in which none of this information is shared is a wasted opportunity.

Once your book is ready for market, sit down with your publicist and/or your marketing team and hash out your talking points and sound bites. Learn them so well that you can easily integrate them into any conversation. Revisit them frequently to make sure they are still relevant and timely.

2. **Presentation (physical appearance, tone, and pace)** – Whether it's for television, radio, print, or an event, if you are live and in view of the public, you always want to look your best!

   › Choose a professional outfit that is appropriate for each particular venue. Wear solids on television whenever possible.

   › Practice good hygiene!

> › Don't forget to smile! It helps you appear warm and friendly, rather than stoic and stand-offish.

3. **Etiquette** – The world of journalism and media is a tight-knit community. One bad impression can hurt your chances of getting not only a second interview with that outlet, but future engagements at other outlets as well. Here are a few tips to avoid an etiquette mistake:

    > › Be kind to everyone. Whether you are speaking to the receptionist or the host, it is imperative that you be friendly. Oftentimes the person in charge will ask for feedback from everyone who came in contact with you. Plus, today's assistant is tomorrow's boss, so don't chance your future by assuming someone isn't important enough for you to take notice of him or her.

    > › Arrive on time. Being early will get you everywhere! Even if you have to wait, it's better to be on time and considerate of other people's schedules rather than miss your interview completely because you weren't where you needed to be.

> Keep it short and sweet. Whether on air or in print, media outlets only have a limited amount of space for content. Respect their time allotments and keep your answers succinct and to the point (this is why it's so important to develop your talking points ahead of time). In broadcast, never—ever—speak past the end of your countdown clock!

> Send thank-you notes or a gift. Show gratitude after your interview with a handwritten note or small gift (if possible) or a quick email. Again, keep it brief, but be sincere.

Soliciting Early Reviews

Soliciting reviews is an ongoing process, but getting started with early reviews is essential to creating some buzz about your book's availability and reaching potential readers. You should have found some good contacts while doing your market research and forming your super-group, as well as your daily networking and platform maintenance, so now is the time to tap into those who offer reviews of new authors. It is a good idea to contact potential reviewers by email or phone, if possible, to determine their interest in your book.

When you make contact with a reviewer, be sure to

include the following in your email or package if they ask for it over the phone:

- 1–2 copies of the book, unless otherwise noted by the reviewer

- An official letter of introduction

- A sell sheet and/or press release that contains a link to your online press kit

The timing of your submission can really affect how well your book can compete with releases from large publishers, and how much attention your book receives from reviewers. In terms of submissions to publishers, the peak months tend to be October and November (with authors aiming for the holiday season when bookstores make up to half or more of their entire annual sales figures). Thus, October and November are the two *worst* months for a small press or self-published author to send out review copies. The sheer size of the incoming requests for reviews is simply too overwhelming to sort through, and yours will be lost in the hubbub.

The second worst months are April and May, because the top publishers have distinct Spring and Fall seasons and marketing campaigns for each, complete with Spring catalogs and Fall catalogs, preprinted reviewer request forms, and marketing tie-ins for capturing a reviewer's attention.

The best months for soliciting reviews are *January and February for Spring season, and July and August for the Fall season.* March and June are relatively quiet as well and are good months to submit. September is brisk, and December mostly dormant, for obvious reasons.

A quick word about *days* of the week (yes, it actually does make a difference which day of the week your book and request arrive on the reviewer's desk!): Monday is consistently the day of heaviest intake for review copies because UPS doesn't deliver on Saturday, and no shipping companies deliver on Sunday. This means that your review copies—and hundreds of other authors' copies—are in the postal pipelines...and they all show up that same Monday morning.

As the week progresses, the flow of books tends to die down a little, with Saturday tending to have the least number of books arriving (though often Saturday's books are simply stacked and added to Monday's pile).

So, *the two best* days *to have your review copy arrive at a reviewer's office are Thursday and Friday.* The competition between other arriving books and yours is considerably less (around 30 titles, say, instead of the 80+ on Monday, and 50 or so on Tuesday and Wednesday), and this means yours will have a better chance of being seen.

PRE-LAUNCH EVENT

Successful authors begin the hard work of generating sales long before the actual release date of their book. These are known as "pre-orders." You've probably purchased, or at least thought of purchasing, a book, film, or CD from a favorite artist long before it came out, to make sure you got your copy before they sold out. The idea is the same here.

One method of collecting these pre-orders is to set up a pre-order button on your website. During the pre-order process, the customers will be prompted to fill in their basic info and make a payment through the website for the book (or books) they order. One way to get people interested enough to pre-order instead of wait until the release date is by offering signed copies or to match Amazon's pricing.

You might want to consider creating a dedicated landing page for pre-orders, which you can utilize in marketing initiatives to drive consumers to a central location for their purchases. A popular addition is to provide incentive for the customers by giving them access to extra content at no charge with an order, which you display info about on the landing page— once the customer has placed the order, they can be given a code to access the free content. As an author, this content can be a collection of short stories, entry into a giveaway, a relevant workbook, or even just a free eBook version of the book they purchased. One new author offered a simple sketch of one of her characters to anyone ordering within a certain timeframe. This encouraged some readers to forego the cheaper Kindle version and throw down for a hardcover book, just because they liked the example sketch shown!

A different route is to simply send people directly to a retailer such as Amazon to place their order during a specified period, usually immediately following the release of the book. In this case, it's important for your publisher to know at least three weeks in advance how many orders you expect will be placed, so they can ensure that they have an adequate number of books in stock to meet the demand. In general, of course, you should always keep your distributors in the loop about your marketing efforts and results—if you don't, there's a good chance the warehouses will not have enough copies of your book to meet an unexpected surge in demand, and many bookstores are reluctant to backorder.

Regardless of how you collect the pre-orders, the idea is to have a complete record of all customers and their number of orders at the end of your pre-order campaign. One word of caution: If you're hoping to generate thousands of pre-orders and want to use them to make a run at a bestseller list, work with an expert who specializes in handling this type of campaign. A targeted campaign like that requires careful coordination and planning, as well as the ability to process thousands of individual orders in a short time span.

THROW A BOOK-LAUNCH PARTY

You've made it! Everything has been set up for getting your book finished, getting it in front of readers, and giving them an easily accessible way of purchasing your book. With the above steps completed, you're now ready to get that book into bookstores, both on literal and virtual bookshelves.

You now receive your first hard copies of your book—your baby. It's beautiful and shiny and you're ready for everyone to see it, like a new parent.

Why not start things off with a ***book launch party***?

Don't get nervous—it's not all that different from throwing a Super Bowl party. The only difference is that *you* are the attraction.

Why You Should Throw A Book-Launch Party

Why *shouldn't* you? There are a myriad of reasons why I always recommend this event to new authors.

1. **It can provide press coverage** – You've put months or years of your life into writing this book—its publication is an event worthy of celebration! It's also time to focus your efforts on attracting critics, journalists, agents, and bookstore owners who can help you move your career forward. If you can make your book release truly newsworthy, you'll have some

assistance creating excitement from industry folks and the local media.

2. **It helps spread the word** – Yes, you hope your family and friends show up…but if you can attract enough attention for the event, there's a good chance you'll have the opportunity to earn new readers and fans—fans who will recommend your book to their friends, who will recommend it to their friends, and so on.

3. **It puts your writing life into context** – Writing is hard work, both the process itself and the emotional ups and downs you experience. Sometimes your friends, family, and colleagues just don't understand. A book-launch party is the perfect opportunity to showcase not just your work but your quirks, life philosophy, methodology, and behind-the-scenes dramatic moments of your writing career so far. Now you can show the people closest to you that there is a method to your madness—but that you also appreciated their patience and faith in you.

4. **It reminds you to have fun** – Let's not forget the basics here. The fact that you are having a book-launch party *because you're now a published author* is one of the biggest achievements of your life—live a little!

The Venue

"Okay," you may be thinking, "I'll try this party thing...but where do I host it?"

The obvious answers are either a bookstore or your own home.

A bookstore—a Barnes and Noble or your local independent store, perhaps—will lend an air of literary credibility to the event. Local media may be more inclined to cover your book-launch if it is tied in with an established bookseller—plus you'll be able to call upon some of that retailer's promotional resources like event calendars, in-store posters, website, email newsletters, etc. On the flip side, though, you will be confined to their space, rules, timeline, and agenda.

If you really want to be comfortable, you could host the event in your home, decorate as you see fit, and blather to your heart's content. The drawbacks to this approach, of course, would be potentially limited space, cleanup, lack of appeal to those outside of your circle and the media, and the fact that you may feel awkward about promoting yourself and your book in your own home. Some people end up feeling like what they're really doing is just entertaining guests and rambling on about themselves.

These are not your only two options, though. Libraries are always a possibility, or you could rent an event space or a park facility. Better yet, find a space that is compatible with the theme or topic of your book, and cross-promote with them.

For instance, if you've written a nautical adventure novel, host your party at a yacht club or boating store. Written a book about early motherhood? Party down in the local birthing center or childcare center. Written the untold history of the Gemini Program? Maybe you should partner up with the closest science museum. The possibilities really are endless, if you just think outside the box a bit.

The Preparation

Preparing for the party is easy—really!—if you follow these simple steps.

1. **Approach the desired venue with your idea**. Be prepared with your press kit and pitch, and tell them why this book launch is not only good for you but also how it will bring new business to their store or new interest to their cause. They'll also want to know how many people you think you can bring out to the party, so have a good estimate. Be sure to include appetizers in your discussion. Everyone likes free food.

2. **Work with the event space on a promotional plan**. Divvy up responsibilities wherever possible, or at the very least have

a discussion that outlines all the promotional activities you plan to do beforehand. They'll see you're serious, and you'll have a plan to execute.

3. **Enlist help.** Find some folks to help out with food, decorations, music, parking, any costumes and props, and other fun features you're planning for. And yes, family and friends are always a good place to start. Also see if local caterers, bands, and other local businesses would be interested in sponsoring you or assisting somehow. It's also a good idea to find another author, a book critic, or other well-known personality to act as a kind of informal MC. They can handle your brief introduction at the beginning of the event and provide a great endorsement for you. See who you can get to donate door prizes as well. Readers love free stuff.

4. **Do promotions.** You may go on a book tour in the future and have ongoing readings and signings as your book gains recognition, but you're never going to have another *launch* for this book, so get it right! Invite friends, family, and fans via email, phone, and through social networks, reminding them of the book-launch party

and asking them for help in spreading the word. Create a Facebook event, and tweet and blog about your preparations and what people can expect. Shoot a video invitation and put it on YouTube. Make it sound fun!

Make sure to design fliers and posters and hang them in coffee shops, libraries, bookstores, and community centers. Let the press know at least two months in advance by sending them a succinct but exciting press release, along with a press kit. "The press" in this case includes not only regional newspapers, but also local art papers, weekly rags, literary journals and reviews, colleges and universities (and individual professors who can inform their students), radio stations (try local NPR affiliates, community radio, and college radio), book bloggers, cable access channels, local TV news broadcasters, and news magazines—just about anyone you can think of!

5. **Follow up**. Keep a detailed spreadsheet of all the people and media outlets you've contacted, along with their contact info and date of first contact. Follow up with them in a couple weeks, asking if they've received your press release and if they will be covering the event. See if there's anything you

can do to accommodate them. Interviews? Free book giveaway? Contributions to their blogs or publications in exchange for coverage?

Make sure to follow up a second time as the event nears. Sometimes scheduled stories are dropped or deadlines are missed, and your event may be the perfect last-minute addition to fill some dead space.

The Party Itself

So, what do you actually *do* when the party's set to start?

First, it's good to remember that although you're the star of the evening, people's attention spans are short. No one likes a conceited egomaniac or wants to listen to you read your work for an hour. Keep things on time, to the point, and allow for a little leisure time at the end for those people who like to linger. Below is a sample guideline:

7:30pm – Doors open. Be there to meet and greet your guests. Put your assistants on snack and drink duty, and make sure the music is at a good level. Make sure to smile!

7:50pm – Get composed. Sneak off to calm the nerves and use the restroom (yes, force yourself to go beforehand. Public speaking does strange things to your waste-management system!). Look at yourself in the mirror and remember the long, hard journey to get here. You've finally made it! Time to share that journey with your family and guests.

8:00pm – Official start time. Your guests should have all arrived; any latecomers will just have to suffer evil glares. If you're hosting in a bookstore or other public venue, the store owner, manager, or events coordinator will announce that things are underway and thank folks for coming. They'll probably talk a bit about their venue, announce upcoming events, and then finally, introduce your selected MC. (If you're hosting the party yourself, a spouse, friend, or colleague can handle this initial welcome.)

8:02pm – The introduction. You don't want to brag about yourself, so your MC takes care of that for you. They get up and sing your praises for two to three minutes, building anticipation and seeking to transition this audience from a group of family, friends, and acquaintances into adoring fans.

8:05pm – You're on! If you're particularly adept at public speaking, you can weave your time between actual readings and recitations from the book, anecdotes, asides, back stories, personal confessions, and more. If you're not, work the personal details of your story into the first 5-10 minutes. Then you can use the remaining time to read straight from your work.

8:30pm – Q&A A lot of people assume that because they'll probably know most of the attendees, a question and answer session seems lame. Oftentimes, though, a reading allows folks who know you quite well to see a different side of you; they get curious and tend to ask questions because they genuinely want to have a discussion with you about these new revelations, not just because they're being polite.

And, if you tend to get nervous thinking about Q&A's, remember that it's a perfectly good answer to say, "I don't know. I'll have to think about that one for a bit; I'll put the answer up on my blog when I've figured it out!" You can also keep extra gifts on hand for those pesky great-question askers. "A cookie for the gentleman who has stumped me with his great questions!"

8:45pm – Conclusion. You and/or the MC can do a raffle drawing and then thank everyone for attending. If you want the party to rage on afterwards, go all night! Folks will appreciate being released from their official responsibilities, and then you can all unwind together.

The Ultimate Rule

Keep a positive attitude.

You can act all incognito if you want, mysterious, cool, gregarious, funny, sarcastic, but be kind to your attendees. Show genuine appreciation for *them* and they'll care about you in return. Plus, you never know who "they" may be—a critic, a blogger…an acquisitions editor who is in town visiting. Perhaps your next number one fan!

GET YOUR BOOK IN BOOKSTORES

You thought the work was over, didn't you? Surprise—there's more you can still do to drum up initial sales.

Whether you've self-published or published traditionally, you have to create a plan and persevere in it in order to keep your book on those shelves. While your book may not turn into a bestseller, you will have the satisfaction of a serious readership and local representation for your work, and there's nothing like seeing your book sitting on a bookshelf for the entire world to see!

Getting the book into bookstores isn't as challenging as you might think, provided that you have done all the steps outlined in the previous chapters. Two things to note about bookstores, however:

- Books that are listed as Print On Demand (POD) are non-refundable. This can limit some bookstores' interest, as they do not want to be stuck with merchandise they cannot return. They may accept a few books, but you will need to get the word out locally that your book is in stock if you want them to order more.

- Books sold by your distributor or publisher traditionally can be returned for a refund within about 90 days. Some stores will return product, only to turn around and buy it again.

Here are some ways you can influence bookstores to get, and keep, your book in stock:

1. **Make sure to start promoting your book via your marketing strategy** *before* **you start contacting bookstores.** This will show them you are serious about your writing career. Then continue promoting it and directing potential customers to the stores that have agreed to stock your book. Also consider:

   › Creating a website or blog specifically for that book

   › New ways to use or places to send your digital press kit

   › Sending press releases to local newspapers and bookstores—it will be much more effective if you send these to individual contact personnel, so do some research to find the specific person who reviews books for each company

   › Advertising in local publications, like book club newsletters or coffee shop periodicals—make sure to let your bookstore contacts know you're marketing the book locally

› Offering to put an "Available at" reference in future ads if the bookstore will accept the book for sale

› Contacting local TV and radio stations for interviews

› Offering to hold author readings at libraries and writing conferences to increase your visibility

› Creating flyers containing information about your book for distribution on public bulletin boards to create local interest

› Attending publishing trade shows held by national and local booksellers associations. Hand out a business card for the book and your contact information; follow up with a PR packet if they show interest. Trade shows also give you the opportunity to meet buyers, distributors, and others working in the publishing and book-selling fields who can offer advice as to how to get a self-published book into bookstores.

> › Asking your friends, neighbors, family, and co-workers to request the book at their local bookstores. Also, resist the temptation to sell the book to them yourself! Ask them to wait to buy it from the store so that there is a history of good sales.

2. **If you are distributing your book on your own, ask the bookstore you're looking at who handles their "consignment" or "local author" books.** Start with chain bookstores to get experience with the process, and then approach independent or single-owner bookstores, which most likely have a large local authors section. They are also more likely to accept your book as a community service, since much of your marketing is probably local promotion. Ask if you can make an appointment to come in and show them the book.

3. **If your book is available through national distributors (such as Ingram or Baker & Taylor), this may sway bookstores just through your initial phone call, since the bookstores can order directly from the distributor.** Taking books one at a time on consignment from the author, however, is much more time-consuming—and

less profitable—for bookstores than going through an established distributor, which automates reordering, returns, and payments.

4. **Be respectful when you meet your bookstore contact(s).** Although you may be a long-time customer of the store, you are now the seller and they are the customer. It's perfectly legitimate to say how much you love the bookstore, as long as you're not pressuring them to take your book simply because you've bought a lot of books from them in the past.

    › Be prepared to leave a copy with the manager or buyer for their evaluation, but only if they ask. Let them know you will be available for author signings and readings when the time comes (aka "when the book sells").

    › I recommend that you do *not* ask to leave a copy, because if they are interested they will ask for it themselves. If you must ask, however, ***do not ask them to read it***—they will read your book if they are interested in it! You have already disobeyed me once by asking to leave your book—please don't do it again!

› Marketing and display decisions are made by the bookstore, and only amateurs ask to be placed on the store's top-selling, most-visible locations before there is a history of strong sales. Don't ask for it.

› Check back periodically with the stores that have taken the book and ask if they need more copies—six to eight weeks is sufficient.

› Don't be begrudging when your contract time is up and the store asks you to take back unsold copies. They took a chance, and if the book didn't sell it is largely because the author didn't promote well or send people in to look at it. If you're cheerful and respectful, though, the bookstore will be much more likely to accept future work from you.

› Distinguish yourself from other authors by being professional, respectful, and easy to work with.

› If you're in a busy bookstore, ***get in and out as quickly as you can***. It's counterproductive to monopolize staff time by continually "selling" yourself and the book. Like every other reader, your bookstore contacts will take a quick look at the book and make their own reading and buying decisions.

5. **Once you've gotten your book into bookstores, don't stop working.** Push the book as hard as you did before to get people to buy. Your book will be restocked, especially by larger chain bookstores, only if sales are good. Let your people know where your book is available locally, and get your supporters to buy them out!

STEP 6

KEEP THE MOMENTUM

WHEN YOUR BOOK first launches, you are excited and motivated to share with everyone you meet. You have spent lots of energy on preparation and marketing using ideas you found in this book, so what do you do now? There are tactics you can reuse, from blog tours, forum posts, interviews, and guest posts, to tweets, Facebook updates, and advertising campaigns, yet most likely your book is not climbing to the top of the Amazon sales rankings or bestsellers lists. That can lead to your own interest waning and it's critical to your career that you keep the momentum! It's possible to "win" the slow-and-steady way, too, especially if you're committed to making a career of writing and publishing as an authorpreneur.

So, how do you keep your sales rolling in, month after month, year after year? This chapter provides ways to keep your book fresh, and references new ways to utilize the social media tools mentioned in Steps 3 & 4. The first and best way to keep your momentum going is to start, continue working on, or finish your next project. The key to making writing your business: never stop writing. Along with continuing to market your old work, you should always be planning and writing something new to keep your entrepreneurial momentum going. It's also important to keep fans connected to your new project, and to get your readers to sign up for your newsletter and follow you on Facebook, Twitter, and your blog so that you can get in touch with them when you have a new release. Don't assume people will just know that you have a new book out and buy it without any input from you.

POST-LAUNCH STRATEGIES

As an authorpreneur, your work is not finished just because you have officially launched your book and it's available for sale. The savvy author thinks of the launch as a starting point. A beginning. You have to assume the role of Chief Marketing Officer (CMO) for your books, because that's what you are—and the job *starts* when the book launches. To be an effective CMO, you have to know what's working and what's not. You can't do that until you have put in the proper amount of time to implement a *post-launch strategy*.

Now we will create a post-launch strategy that will allow you to evaluate your business and marketing plan, implement new strategies as needed, and develop the process for your "rinse-and-repeat." There is no perfect process, but you should always be working to ensure you are putting your best foot forward.

Here are some quick ideas for your post-launch strategy:

1. **Write/publish another book!** Publishing your next book is extremely important for an authorpreneur, especially if you are writing a series. You can discount the first one heavily, or make the eBook free with KDP select, which then drives sales of all future books. It also makes your efforts twice as profitable – i.e., talking to a bookstore, doing a signing, attending a book fair, etc.

2. **Evaluate your first week and your first month of sales.** Look for patterns in your sales as you move forward, but this initial evaluation may tell you a lot about how your pre-launch marketing strategies worked.

3. **Engage in high-result/low-time-investment marketing tactics.** Many authors have seen great success using advertising with BookBub, Freebooksy, EBookBooster, and Pixel of Ink. See Appendix B for a list of eBook promotion sites that I have seen authors use. It is not a complete list, but it's a great place to start!

4. **Create short videos and post them on YouTube, your website, and social media.** These videos can be recorded using any device, but you should:

    › Make sure you look decent

    › Keep it short and sweet—15 seconds or less

    › Be sure to include a link to buy your book or sign up for your newsletter as a description or in the comments section

5. **Engage daily in social media, including online groups.** Always work on connecting with your audience. Remember that you can automate some of your posts to auto-post to various profiles and to give you a level of interaction, without taking up hours of each day.

6. **Write a new blog post or post a portion of your new work.** You should also comment on blog posts about a topic of interest to your target audience.

7. **Reach out to media.** Contact a reporter to comment on a story and/or introduce yourself as a potential source for a follow-up story. An easy way to do this is by signing up at HelpAReporter.com, from which you

will receive daily emailed leads; be sure to follow up quickly since they usually have same-day deadlines.

8. **Write and distribute another press release.** This should not just be another introduction to your book; the key is to find something current to tie to your latest release. See an example here:

THE INNER SOCIETY: NEW NOVEL ADDRESSES UNSPOKEN TEEN ISSUES IN CHRISTIAN LITERATURE

Today's high schools are frightening battlegrounds of cyber bullying and gun violence. Teens are inundated by pop culture's contradicting messages about sexuality, religion, and success. Even when schools seem to be relatively positive environments, the powerful peer pressure to fit in can also cause many teens to be terrified of school.

In THE INNER SOCIETY (Ellechor Publishing House/March 2013), a recently released Christian Young Adult novel series by Melinda L. Bohannon, Norfolk High School in Virginia becomes the playground of a powerful society of rich and spoiled teenagers who believe they are inherently better than everyone else is. That is, until Maggie Kraus, a rebellious and troubled teen, comes to Norfolk. When she blatantly challenges the balance of power, she becomes their next target. Will she survive the deadly game that follows?

Fans of the Twilight and Hunger Games trilogies, and any teen who has suffered adversity and heartbreak, will love the intense drama and suspense in Bohannon's new series of novels, based on the true lives and stories of teenagers the author encountered in her 20 years of dedication to teaching, youth advising, and foster parenting. Bohannon wrote the series with an intentionally secular tone, yet grounded the books in life-giving values so it could serve as a powerful tool for youth advisors and parents desperate to reach struggling teens who do not normally accept guidance from adults.

Drugs, pre-marital sex, abortion, pornography, and other timely issues often inadequately examined in Christian literature are carefully addressed through the experiences of the characters. In a recent interview Bohannon said, "If Christians won't get out of their comfort zones and venture out into the streets to reach teenagers in their own territory – they will not reach them at all." She hopes that THE INNER SOCIETY will inspire a new generation of writers who will not be afraid to deal with the heavy issues that teens face today in a world of rapidly declining values.

THE INNER SOCIETY can be purchased online at most major retailers, including Amazon.com, Barnes & Noble and Powell's Books. Get a copy for the high school student near you, today!

---

9. **Pitch yourself as a speaker** to local trade associations, groups, and events, if that's something you are comfortable doing. If not, don't worry; you will work up to that for future books!

10. **Pitch yourself to an internet radio program.** Once again, only if you are comfortable! My favorite websites to search for programs to pitch to, in addition to HelpAReporter, are RadioGuestList.com and BlogTalkRadio's main website. On BTR I simply search by the genre/category of my book, and I also do a search for exclusive author shows that don't specify a genre.

11. **Find the people who are supporting you (your fans), embrace them, and *thank* them.** Say "Thank You!" early and often, and mean it. That's really all there is to it when it comes to continually driving new sales.

12. **Have fun!** If you view marketing as work that you resent, guess what kind of results will follow? But if you decide to embrace it and celebrate small victories, you might

find that you actually enjoy the work—
and the rewards.

RETHINK BOOK TOURS

Upon publication of a book, many authors begin to fantasize about the wildly successful book tour they wish to embark on, envisioning miles of lines of eager readers and hours of engaging conversation. Unfortunately, that's just not the case in most scenarios. I generally advise authors that a book tour should not be on a top ten to-do list when it comes to marketing a book. For those authors with large platforms and extra resources, however, a book tour can still make a lot of sense. Especially if it's done right.

Author tours are evolving, and a 30-minute reading followed by a signing just will not cut it anymore; people just aren't interested like they used to be, and honestly, you probably won't sell more than a few books.

On the other hand, here's a best-case scenario that combines a creative book tour with cross-promotion, which we will talk more about in Step 7: Pay It Forward. Sci-fi and fantasy author Neil Gaiman and his wife, musician Amanda Palmer, went on tour together. They created a vague, goofy, and charming video to build awareness and raise funds to help them book larger venues and print merchandise in advance. Gaiman and Palmer's Kickstarter campaign not only fueled buzz about their tour, but it convinced 3,873 people to donate a combined total of \$133,341—about 7 times what they requested.

Now, even if you are not a well-established, multi-award-winning writer who is married to a rock star, you can take a few lessons away from Gaiman and Palmer's tour strategy.

1. **Do your own promotions.** Hopefully the bookstore will advertise for your event by putting signs in the store and notices on their website, but there's no guarantee this will happen, so advertise on your own website, your blog, Twitter, Facebook, and anything else you have access to. Make sure everyone who likes you knows what's going on, including where and when the event will take place. No one wants to or should ever bank on opportunity sales—sales from people who just stumble by and decide they want a book. Attracting random shoppers is possible, but those readers will be much more likely to join a crowd of entertained people than to sit in an empty group of chairs.

2. **Plan something truly interesting for your audience.** Come prepared with a presentation, speech, special music, or something else that will keep your audience captivated. While you can do a brief reading,

that should never comprise the bulk of your time. Similarly, Q&A's are great, but don't rely on them. What's interesting to readers is the information authors can provide that they can't get anywhere else. If you want to try something new, come with questions for your audience. What did they like (and, if you're brave and thick-skinned, what did they not like)? Are there things they want to know more about? What made them pick up your book in the first place? Their answers will provide some of the most insightful and accurate market research on your book, and will keep the audience interested and engaged.

3. **Have the basic Q&A answers ready beforehand.** Where did you get your inspiration? How hard was it to get published? Did you meet with a lot of resistance? Who are your characters based on? How did you get started in your field? All of these are common questions at author readings, so be ready with the answers so you can keep the event moving at a swift pace.

4. **Bring backup in the form of a colleague or talented acquaintance.** Gaiman's event didn't just involve him reading an excerpt. He brought someone with him who drew

her own audience. If you have a friend, colleague, or acquaintance who can reach a different crowd and even slightly relate to your topic, bring him and make sure he advertises to all of his fans as well. This is also helpful because it attracts additional business to the event, making the venue more likely to host you again and support you in the future. This is the beauty of cross-promotion; it's a gift that keeps giving.

Much like publishing a book, going on a book tour is a marathon, not a sprint. In order to have a successful event, you need to take the time to promote your appearance, prepare in advance, and wow your audience. Don't be afraid to get creative and initiate a Kickstarter or IndieGoGo campaign, if appropriate. The most important thing to remember is to make your reading more than a reading. Give people a reason to show up, stay, and become lifelong fans of your work.

BOOK BUY BOMB (AKA "BUY MY BOOK DAY")

The *book buy bomb* is a relatively new and progressive marketing technique that involves encouraging your fan base to consolidate its purchasing power into one day to increase your chances of making it onto a bestsellers list. When you get many people to buy a book on the same day on Amazon specifically, it causes a rise in the Amazon Sales Rank and can propel a book onto the Amazon Bestsellers list. Sales on Amazon are monitored by all the major bookstores, so a sudden spike will help the book to be noticed by bookstores as well as media.

The most important thing to know before you run off to schedule a "bomb" is that having a solid fan base and being able to mobilize them, in addition to having a great product, is the best way to succeed with this type of strategy. If you are a first time author and looking to create a "bomb" that will allow you to rise to meteoric success in a single afternoon (which is after all, The American Dream), it probably won't work quite like that. The best you can hope for is an increased awareness of your title that temporarily boosts additional sales and that you can continue to build on with other marketing techniques.

However, if you have a few titles under your belt or even just a bit of a fan base, it should only help. Here are three key tips to help you get started:

1. Pick a day with significance: your birthday, the anniversary of your first published book, etc.

2. Ask sincerely with a minimal amount of pressure on the request

3. Reach out to as many people as possible

Remember, *a successful "bomb" does* not *mean you are a bestselling author* in real life. Only consistent sales and high ratings can do that over a longer period. A successful "bomb" brings greater exposure of your book to potential readers, gives you something to brag modestly about, and can help you push your marketing plans into high gear.

ATTEND LOCAL FAIRS & EVENTS

In a post-launch world you should have a list of all—and I mean *every*—local event where you can promote or sell your book. Do not just look for the usual suspects: book fairs, library events, etc. You want to seek out the non-traditional ways you can market and sell your book locally. If you have a particularly cool car mentioned in your book, you could search for car shows and see if you can get a booth. Do any of your characters have a favorite hobby mentioned regularly in the book? Find a convention. You should also look for things that interest you personally; it is very likely your book may have some crossover to help you make your selling points. If you have written a business book, seek out speaking engagements at local entrepreneur or Chamber of Commerce meetings. Check out the starter list in Appendix C to help you get started.

You must always stay current with local events and the success rates of your implemented strategies in order to keep your book relevant. This type of forward motion will help you tweak future launches, keep your book sales up, and even increase them so you are making a profit. All chances of success diminish when you become stagnant, so keep the momentum!

PAY IT FORWARD

Now, THIS IS the part where authors sometimes forget their beginnings and go for solo-glory. Reaping what you sow is not just something silly your parents made up to punish you. It's real! Consider the saying "He's not heavy, he's my brother!" As you have moved through the publishing process and promoted your own work, you have undoubtedly come across various authors in your field. While you may be tempted to only use them to convince others to buy your books, remember the major rule for working with your author super-group: Provide value.

Now that you have launched, you should start thinking about tangible ways to provide value for your brothers and sisters in publishing, such as:

- **Rounding up resources.** Round up books, websites, and other resources on topics related to yours and then add them to your home page. Be helpful to others, and they will send people to you.

- **Boosting others**. Help a fellow author or a first-timer buzz his outstanding new book, class, service, or conference. If you are a believer, become an evangelist. Moreover, if you really mean it, offer a testimonial.

- **Offering your services.** According to Gary Vaynerchuk's book *Crush It!*, the best question you can ever ask on social media is, "What can I do for you?" Such a simple idea, yet so profoundly intelligent. Put it to work for you on a regular basis.

- **Being a good guest.** Ask yourself the hard-hitting questions others do not dare ask (but are dying to know). Now you have a compelling guest post to share on your "Freebies" page.

- **Hitting the highlights.** You do not have to give the play-by-play after you attend an event, but share the best of what you noticed or learned. You can even go multimedia with your coverage. Have your camera, audio recorder, and video recorder ready to grab snippets of live action to share with others who wish they could have been there.

A ***cross-promotion campaign*** addresses all of the above outlined ways to give back. By making an agreement with five to six authors to cross-promote, you are creating value for all parties, offering services, boosting others, and gathering resources. Ellechor Media hosted a company book launch for three of our authors in Portland, Oregon, that heavily utilized cross-promotion to get in front of our local audience. We not only invited other local authors with Christian books releasing in the same month to participate in the book-signing, we engaged with local businesses and a small business in Los Angeles for sponsorships in exchange for marketing. We also invited representatives from the local Start Making a Reader Today organization to host a booth for donations. Overall, we were told it was the "classiest book launch" some guests had ever been to, and we sold three times as many books as we would have on our own.

CROSS-PROMOTION RULES & BENEFITS

Cross-promotion works best when you create groupings of books that are likely to be purchased by the same reader, often similar in style and genre, sometimes even by the same author. Collections of five or six books are most effective. Any more than that and the marketing becomes unwieldy; any fewer and promotion and sales opportunities could be lost.

If the reader is looking for action, all the books

within the group need to kick some booty. If the reader is looking for Christian publications, the books should be free of foul language and questionable romance scenes.

Cross promotion does not always have to involve books in the same genre, however. What if you only have one or two adventure titles? Books in similar sub-genres or that have similar threads can be grouped together within an event, catalog, or even back-of-book ads. For example, one reader might enjoy the action of an adventure novel while another might enjoy the mystery—both adventure and mystery/suspense books can be featured with proper identification of the genre change.

How Cross-Promotion Creates Sales

The rules for marketing in the case of cross-promotion are the same as always: great cover art, exciting quotes, and a brief overview. This kind of marketing has been shown by Amazon research to be far more effective at generating sales than prose in the back matter, which turns off readers. (The back matter is the section at the end of a book, usually with one blank page to separate it.)

Each promo should drive the reader to the book's Amazon product page. Let the reader sample or buy there rather than muddling through long sections of prose in your back matter.

You will find that by making these deals with other

authors who are releasing books around the same time you will not only develop a great give-and-take relationship with that author, but you are building a reputation in the author community. By sowing the spirit of collaboration and support, you will find that many more opportunities will be revealed to you. By neglecting to pay it forward, you are likely limiting yourself by becoming the sole promoter for your book. Giving your time to others can be just as advantageous for yourself as it is for the author you are helping promote. You will start reaping what you have sown! You can cross-promote other authors and start paying it forward by:

- Interviewing other authors on your blog

- Promoting your publishing team on social media sites

- Offering copies of books to charity programs

Create Your Campaign

To get started, create a list of similar authors, their book titles, and complimentary items that you can use throughout your campaign. Connect with the authors/vendors to create a cross promotion agreement that works for all of you. You will want to have at least 2-3 partners, but there is no limit as long as you plan a campaign long enough to feature every item.

Design the Timeline

First off, you will need to construct a timeline that allows you to feature each contribution and collaborating author. You can plan for one or all of the following as a part of your campaign:

- Bonus gift offers from your partners
- Email/e-zine (electronic magazine) blasts
- Twitter campaign
- A contest
- Virtual blog tour

There are different strategies, technical aspects, and creative elements to each of these components which would take too long to discuss here. For now, let's say that you decided you were going to utilize all of them in some way.

Coordinate Your Materials

Assuming you have already determined the level of commitment promised from your partners, your next step would be to gather relevant materials from them, such as a headshot, bio, and bonus material information, including a link to the opt-in page where people will sign up to receive their gift.

A word of advice: It is highly likely you will need to guide many of your partners as to what is an appropriate bonus gift. A good bonus gift should be a downloadable entry-level gift. You do not want them to offer any gifts that require the customer to buy something else to receive it, or requires them to travel to a specific geographic location. If they are offering free or discounted coaching or consultation, make sure they include parameters such as saying the offer is limited to the first 15 people who sign up. Without a limit, if they have a high number of requests, they might find it impossible to honor them all. You, as the manager of your campaign, need to guide your partners to choosing the right kind of gift.

As you collect this information, make sure you use some sort of tracking system to cross check and verify that you have received all the info.

Create Your Pre-Launch Page and Follow-Ups

Next, you will need to assemble all your partner information, along with key info about you and your book, onto a campaign landing page. On this page, people will find out about you, your book, the date of the event, and the bonus gift offerings. Make sure you standardize the format in which you will publish partner content on the web, so everyone's entry looks similar.

Apart from the partner information, the key ingredient on this page is a sign-up form, where they will sign up to receive a reminder about the promotional event. This sign-up form should be connected to an auto-responder that sends them a follow-up message saying something to the effect of, *"Thanks for your interest in my book. I'll be sending you a reminder the day before the campaign starts so you can get those great bonus gifts you read about. Be sure to mark your calendar!"*

Create Promo Copy

The next thing you will need to do is create some great promotional copy for your partners to use for your campaign. Prepare these three types of promo copy:

- **Newsletters/e-zine articles** – You can make two contrasting pieces of e-zine copy for your partners per month to give them diversity and choice (they are likely to send only one per month).

- **Tweets (for Twitter)** – You can make 50-100 tweets for partners, making sure they are 120 characters or less. It's really not as complex as it might sound, and it can make your campaign vibrant, fun, and very effective. The last 20 characters you will need for you or your partners to provide a link to your newsletter, landing page, or website.

- **Virtual interviews** (if you are planning to do a virtual blog tour) – A virtual interview is when your blog tour hosts send you a few questions in advance before the date of their stop on your tour. You answer the questions either in written format or via podcast, and they are posted on the scheduled date.

CREATE CLEAR INSTRUCTIONS

The last step to getting your campaign off the ground is to create a set of clear, written instructions for your partners. Always include a timeline, a description of the components, and a breakdown of how everything will run. Write it in such a way that it is visually easy to read, and convert it into a PDF document. Give them tips on how to use the materials and how to increase traffic to their advantage.

BLIND DATE WITH A BOOK

This is a newer campaign concept and a great way to exercise some cross-promotional strategy. All you need are willing authors who will allow their books to be given away or sold at rock-bottom prices. The idea is to draw readers in with a new hook. This time, it's less about one specific book and more of a call for book lovers to take a chance on some new reading material. Who knows? They might end up discovering their new favorite author. Use the guide below to plan your own BDWAB cross-promotion campaign.

1. **Find a location and pick a date.** A library or independent bookstore may be willing to participate and even donate books that they planned to give away. If they offer books, remember to keep it limited, since the idea is to feature you and your partners.

2. **Each book should be wrapped in brown paper** with about 3-4 lines of general promo text to give readers an idea of what they are getting into. The promo lines are best if there is a price tag to allow readers just a little more information to help make a decision, without giving away too much. The price should never be more than $5, and I would suggest setting it at $1. For a free giveaway, I recommend only labeling them by genre to keep the mystery alive.

3. **Create a promotional launch page or website to promote the event.** You will highlight the books and their authors who will attend.

4. **Plan a brief agenda.** You can include games like "Guess the Author" for attendees to link information featured on the website with each attending author. You can also have a book signing table set up for those not willing to take a risk and

for those who have already selected their book to get the author's signature.

Continue to think of different ways to adapt your previous strategies to include other authors and even consultants or vendors. By always providing value and paying it forward, you are creating a network of people who not only are more likely to purchase your book themselves, but who are also more likely to recommend it to friends and family. These people will become your ambassadors without any uncomfortable prodding from you, because they see you not as a salesperson but as someone who is credible and worthy.

Your Own Bookshop

One of the most creative marketing ideas I heard about (thanks to one of my authors) was the concept of opening a bookstore of nothing but your book! Walter Swan, a plasterer-turned-author, first opened the One Book Bookstore in Bisbee, Arizona after self-publishing a compilation of stories about his life that publishers had rejected. Then, Andrew Kessler sublet a storefront for a couple of months and only sold his book, *Martian Summer: Robot Arms, Cowboy Spacemen, and My 90 Days with the Phoenix Mars Mission* (Pegasus, 2011). Andrew had shelves and shelves full of the one title. It was also under "staff picks" and "book of the month." The discovery of

Andrew's store led to a lot of media attention and, subsequently, hundreds of book sales.

This is not the business model I would recommend, but may I suggest "your own bookshop" with a twist? Turn it into a cross-promotion campaign! Find a retail space that could use the attention or one that hasn't been able to rent out space in a while. Collaborate with other local authors and "starving artists" to create a temporary themed pop-up shop. With additional press releases, media contact, and other marketing efforts, this could turn into a highly profitable (short-term) venture.

CONCLUSION

THE SEVEN STEPS I have taken you through cover your author-entrepreneurial journey from book concept to post-publication, but this is just the beginning! Repeat these steps every time you launch a new book, building on the work you were able to do on your first pass. The primary goal of this book is to help you, as an author, find a place to start in your entrepreneurial endeavors. Turning your writing career into a full-fledged business is not an easy task, but following these steps will help you turn your initial motivation into tangible results you can build on.

Questions to Always Ask Yourself

As you review your publishing and marketing plans and look to the future of your publications, make sure to answer these five basic questions every time:

1. Who is my target audience?

2. What is the value of my book for my audience?

3. Where are the readers who would find my book most useful?

4. How can I engage with them in a meaningful way?

5. Who can I collaborate with to maximize value for my readers?

Once you can answer these questions with a certain accuracy, you will become more effective in your book publishing and marketing process. The key is to recognize that you are your number one fan, promoter, and investor. Once you take ownership of your writing, as I have led you through in this book, you will be able to make more money while doing what you love.

One Last Word on Marketing...

Once you get going, there is a "snowball effect" that occurs in marketing. The more you market yourself and your titles, the easier and more efficient it should become. To put it another way, every copy sold makes it easier to sell the next one. This is especially true at Amazon, where your sales ranking is influenced by a wide variety of factors. Understanding Amazon's recent algorithms is key to creating several weeks of consistently high rankings, but that is a long chapter in another book. I would recommend the following to boost your Amazon eBook publishing and marketing knowledge:

1. Justen James' *Boost Your Kindle Success: Real Strategies to Supercharge Your eBook Sales on Amazon*

2. Bill Pottle's *Sell More With Amazon Kindle Analytics: How to Optimize eBook Sales*

You may think that many of the marketing activities mentioned are not worth time spent; however, while actual results are hard to predict, there is a foundational starting point for all of your publishing activities.

You may delete the first paragraph of your book as fluff in editing, but would you have the book if you had not started there? Marketing a book successfully requires you to start somewhere, and it's always best to start with the basics. You may decide later in Step 6 that certain actions are not working for you, and the data you gathered will help you focus on what does work. You can't know if it works if you have never tried it before.

...And One On Your Author Brand

I would like to reiterate that, as an authorpreneur, *you* are the brand. If there is poor editing, cover design, etc., that reflects on you as an author and as an entrepreneur. While a traditional author may not have a lot of say in the process, you should make sure you signed with a company you trust. Sometimes self-publishing is the best way for you to empower yourself as an author in order to make the best decisions for your product.

Self-publishing used to have a bad stigma, where readers felt you were paying someone to produce your work because your book wasn't "good enough," but now the stigma is rapidly disappearing. Self-publishing is more like just running a small business that happens to be a publishing company, and readers are giving these authors a fair shot in their search for good books.

No matter the path you took, make sure you get involved as much as you can and do your due diligence. If you are asked to edit, then edit! Give feedback on your book cover. At no point should you sit back passively and disengage. Be polite, be able to compromise, and be your brand.

Next Steps

Do not just read this book through once and toss it aside! As you go through your publishing process, go back and review relevant chapters as necessary for your current situation. This guide is the first to take you as an author from concept to execution, and you will need to revisit often to follow up on the actionable instructions included in each step. The result is a blending of the entrepreneurial spirit with writing talent to create a successful business that supports the life you really want.

Being an authorpreneur is not just about writing and publishing books. Remember, in the introduction I said that an authorpreneur does not solely write and promote books. As you investigate campaigns for your last step, "Pay It Forward," think about what you have to offer beyond just your book. What else can you build around your brand? To continue being a true authorpreneur, you must seek new ways to apply these steps and diversify your author platform into areas such as speaking, courses, webinars, audio books, etc. Even if you are not comfortable at first, there are ways to ease yourself into becoming a savvy and successful authorpreneur with multiple streams of income, especially passive income (money you make without much effort). You could write a new book for every season if that is your true desire, but the next phase will allow you to switch things up a bit and keep life interesting.

One example of a heavily diverse authorpreneur is Bill Pottle. He runs his own martial arts studio and literally wrote the book on how to run one. While the book itself may have a small audience, it increases the likelihood that prospective students sign up on the spot since he is seen as an expert on his business. Bill has not stuck to writing only martial arts books, either. He also writes and publishes various short stories and Christian fantasy novels. Even his wife, Kate, is getting in on the action, making them an authorpreneurial family.

The 7-Step Guide to Authorpreneurship was

designed just to get you started, so if you are ready for the next phase then sign up for my newsletter at www.PlanWritePublish.com, where I will be offering additional information on becoming an authorpreneur. You will also have exclusive access to my upcoming workshops and e-courses for a more in-depth journey into the world of an authorpreneur.

Welcome to authorpreneurship!

BIBLIOGRAPHY

Bookmasters. (2012, May 10). *Bookmasters Blog.* Retrieved from Bookmasters: http://blog.bookmasters. com/2012/05/10/5-tips-for-writing-great-book-marketing-copy-simplify-to-maximize/

Chandler, S. (2011, November 3). *Author Postpartum: What Happens After the Book Release Frenzy Fizzles.* Retrieved from Authority Publishing: http://authoritypublishing.com/book-marketing/author-post-partum-what-happens-after-the-book-release-frenzy-fizzles/#sthash. NDIEpM6N.dpuf

Chandler, S. (2013, March 13). *Social Media for Authors: 12 Ways to Leverage LinkedIn for Book Promotion.* Retrieved from Authority Publishing: http://authority-publishing.com/social-media/social-media-for-authors-12-ways-to-leverage-linkedin-for-book-promotion/

Collier, M. (n.d.). *How to Totally Botch a New Book's Marketing In the First Month (Hint: Create a Plan).* Retrieved from Mack Collier: http://www.mackcollier. com/how-to-totally-botch-a-new-books-marketing-in-the-first-month-hint-create-a-plan/

Cox, J. (2008, January 8). *Publication & Review Copy Timing.* Retrieved from Midwest Book Review: http://www.mid-westbookreview.com/bookbiz/advice/revcopy.htm

Diaz, S. (2010, July 1). *How to Manage Author Platform-Building Opportunities.* Retrieved from GreenLeaf Book Group Blog: http://www. greenleafbookgroup.com/blog/2010/07/01/ how-to-manage-author-platform-building-opportunities

Four P's of Christian Marketing. (2007). Retrieved from WordClay: http://www.wordclay.com/genre/christian-fourps.aspx

How to Get a Self Published Book Into Bookstores. (n.d.). Retrieved from WikiHow: http://www.wikihow.com/Get-a-Self-Published-Book-Into-Bookstores

Katz, C. (2011, December 12). *50 SIMPLE WAYS TO BUILD YOUR PLATFORM IN 5 MINUTES A DAY.* Retrieved from Writer's Digest: http://www.writersdigest.com/whats-new/50-simple-ways-to-build-your-platform-in-5-minutes-a-day

King, M. (2012, February 1). *PR Basics for Authors – Tip 1: Create A Digital Press Kit.* Retrieved from BookBaby Blog: http://blog.bookbaby.com/2012/02/pr-basics-for-authors-tip-1-create-a-digital-press-kit/

Luedeke, A. (2013, April 8). *5 Ideas for Using Pinterest as an Author.* Retrieved from Jane Friedman: http://janefriedman.com/2013/04/08/5-ideas-for-using-pinterest-for-authors/

McCray, C. (2011, October 21). *How to Boost Your Online Book Sales With "Sales Nodes".* Retrieved from Digital Book World: http://www.digitalbookworld.com/2011/how-to-boost-your-online-book-sales-with-%E2%80%9Csales-nodes%E2%80%9D/

Meehan, M. (2012, May 10). *Rethinking The Author Tour.* Retrieved from GreenLeaf Book Group: http://www.greenleafbookgroup.com/blog/2012/05/10/rethinking-the-author-tour

Nichol, M. (2011, August 20). *How To Hire An Editor.* Retrieved from Daily Writing Tips: http://www.dailywritingtips.com/how-to-hire-an-editor/

Robley, C. (2011, April 26). *Book Promotion for the Self-Published Author.* Retrieved from BookBaby Blog: http://blog.bookbaby.com/2011/04/book-promotion-for-the-self-published-author/

Robley, C. (2012, March 21). *How to Throw a Book Launch Party That Isn't a Waste of Time.* Retrieved from BookBaby Blog: http://blog.bookbaby.com/2012/03/how-to-throw-a-book-launch-party-that-isnt-a-waste-of-time/

Sears, K. (2011, July 11). *Getting a Jump on Sales with Preorders.* Retrieved from GreenLeaf Book Group Blog: http://www.greenleafbookgroup.com/blog/2011/07/11/getting-a-jump-on-sales-with-preorders

Serafinn, L. (2010, March 22). *5 Steps to Create an Amazon Bestselling Book Campaign.* Retrieved from Spirit Authors: http://spiritauthors.com/news/5-steps-to-create-an-amazon-bestselling-book-campaign/

APPENDIX A

BOOK REVIEWERS

This is not an endorsement of these reviewers, but simply a compiled list of options.

Website Title	Website Link	Genre
A Blog About Nothing	http://cynthial11.blogspot.com	Book Reviews
A Bookish Affair	http://abookishaffair.blogspot.com	Book Reviews; News; Literature
A Bookshelf Monstrosity	http://bookshelfmonstrosity.blogspot.com	Book Reviews
A Lil Dash of Diva	http://www.alildashofdiva.com	Book Reviews; New Product Review; Recipes; Motherhood
A Little Dizzy	http://www.alittledizzy.com	Book Reviews; Computer & Video Games; Technology; Food; Internet; Movies & Video; Television; Toys
A Peek At My Bookshelf	http://deenasbooks.blogspot.com	Book Reviews; Books; Christian
A Striped Armchair	http://astripedarmchair.wordpress.com	Book Reviews; Fiction; Literature
A Taste of Chocolate	http://www.curlychellez.blogspot.com	Book Reviews; Fashion; Lifestyle; Music; Travel; Women's Interests; African American; Hair

Aaron Miller	http://blogs.courier-journal.com/aaronmiller	Book Reviews; Internet; Movies & Video; Television
Afro Nerd	http://afronerd.blogspot.com	Book Reviews; Culture; Religion; Ethnic & Multicultural; Entertainment; African American
Age 30+ ... A Lifetime of Books	http://age30books.blogspot.com	Book Reviews
Amused by Books	http://www.amusedbybooks.com	Book Reviews; News; Literature
Amy Reads	http://amckiereads.com	Book Reviews
ashleymott.com	http://ashleymott.com	Book Reviews; Movies & Video; Music; Television
Autumn Blues Reviews	http://autumnbluesreviews.com	Book Reviews; New Product Review; Sweepstakes & Giveaways
Babbling About Books and More	http://redheadedkb.tumblr.com	Book Reviews; Fiction
Badass Book Reviews	http://nurslings.tumblr.com	Book Reviews
Bed Rest Book Club	http://www.thebedrestbookclub.com	Book Reviews; Family & Parenting; Pregnancy & Birth; Restaurant Reviews
Beth's Book Reviews	http://www.bethsbookreviews.com	Book Reviews

Biblio File	http://www.jenrothschild.com	Book Reviews
Bibliophiliac	http://bibliophiliac-bibliophiliac.blogspot.com	Book Reviews; Fiction; Poetry
Birdbrain(ed) Book Blog	http://birdbrainbb.net	Book Reviews; Fiction; Mystery Books; Non-Fiction; Science Fiction Books
Black Gate Blog	http://www.billwardwriter.com/category/black-gate-blog	Book Reviews; Science Fiction Books
Boekie's Book Review	http://www.boekiesbookreviews.com	Book Reviews; Trading Cards & Comics
Book Blather	http://bookblather.net	Book Reviews; Teen/Young Adult
Book Blog	http://www.stltoday.com/entertainment/books-and-literature/book-blog/	Book Reviews; Authors; Books
Book Buzz	http://www.yorkblog.com/books	Book Reviews
Book by Book	http://books.lohudblogs.com	Book Reviews; Poetry
Book Examiner	http://www.examiner.com/x-562-book-examiner	Book Reviews; Book Publishing; Books
Book Him Danno!	http://bookhimdanno.blogspot.com	Book Reviews; Fiction; Science Fiction Books
Book Jabber	http://blogs.battlecreekenquirer.com/bookjabber	Book Reviews; Literature; Books
Book Pleasures	http://www.bookpleasures.com	Book Reviews; Authors
Book Reviews by Elizabeth A. White	http://www.elizabethawhite.com	Book Reviews

Book Reviews, Fiction Reflections, N' More	http://personalliterarybookfrenzy.blogspot.com	Book Reviews; Fiction
Book Snob	http://booksnob-booksnob.blogspot.com	Book Reviews; Books
Book Trends	http://www.booktrends.org	Book Reviews; Children's Books; Fiction; Teen/Young Adult; Books
Book, Line and Sinker	http://booklineandsinker.com	Book Reviews; News; Literature
Charming Chelsey's	http://dwellinpossibilitybooks.blogspot.com	Book Reviews; Books
Chefdruck Musings	http://www.chefdruck.com	Book Reviews; Children & Youth; Family & Parenting; Food; Movies & Video; Television; Motherhood
Chic Darling	http://add-vodka.com	Book Reviews; Consumer Electronics; Fitness & Exercise; Lifestyle; Travel; Women's Interests; Fashion & Beauty
Chick Lit Teens	http://www.chicklitteens.com	Book Reviews; Teen/Young Adult
Christ is Deeper Still!	http://thegospelcoalition.org/blogs/rayortlund	Christian; Religion; Book Reviews
Christie's Book Reviews	http://www.christiesbookreviews.com	Book Reviews; News; Literature
Confessions of a Book Addict	http://www.confessionsofabookaddict.com	Book Reviews; Fiction; Teen/Young Adult

Contrary Blog	http://blog.contrarymagazine.com	Book Reviews; Literature; Authors; Writing
Cool and Hip, I Am Not.	http://coolandhipiamnot.blogspot.com	Book Reviews; Education; Family & Parenting; Personal Finance; Humor & Satire
Cornucopia of Reviews	http://cornucopiaofreviews.blogspot.com	Book Reviews; Teen/Young Adult
Crossed Purposes	http://crossedpurposes.com	History; Christian; Theology
Crossover	http://www.crossoverbooks.blogspot.com	Book Reviews
Crowding the Book Truck	http://crowdingthebooktruck.blogspot.com	Book Reviews; Children's Books; Fiction; Teen/Young Adult; Non-Fiction
Dad of Divas	http://dadofdivas.com	Book Reviews; Family & Parenting; Fatherhood
Dear Author	http://dearauthor.com	Book Reviews; Fiction; Romance
Dolce Bellezza	http://www.dolcebellezza.net	Book Reviews; Fiction; Literature
Eclectic / Eccentric	http://www.eclectic-eccentric.com	Book Reviews; Fiction; Teen/Young Adult; Literature; Non-Fiction; Science Fiction Books
'Ello Honey Bee	http://www.ellohoneybee.com	Book Reviews; Arts & Entertainment; Fashion; Fiction; Fitness & Exercise; Personal Health; New Product Review; Relationships; Literature; Sweepstakes & Giveaways

Emdashes	http://emdashes.com	Book Reviews; Journalism
Entertainment Examiner	http://www.examiner.com/x-585-entertainment-examiner	Book Reviews; Celebrities; Movies & Video; Television; Theater & Performing Arts; Entertainment; DVD & Video Reviews
Everyday Reading	http://everydayreading.blogspot.com	Book Reviews; Fashion; Cookbooks; Recipes
Ex Libris	http://www.stella-exlibris.com	Book Reviews; Books
Fain Literary Review	http://fainliteraryreview.blogspot.com	Book Reviews; Fiction; Poetry; Literature; Non-Fiction
Fantastic Book Review	http://www.fantasticbookreview.com	Book Reviews
Fantasy Magazine	http://www.fantasy-magazine.com	Book Reviews; Fantasy
Fiction Vixen	http://www.fictionvixen.com	Fiction Book Reviews
Five Alarm Book Reviews	http://fivealarmbookreviews.com	Book Reviews
Flamingo House Happenings	http://flamingohouse.net	Book Reviews; Children's Books
For What It's Worth	http://www.fwiwreviews.net	Book Reviews
From Left to Write	http://www.fromlefttowrite.com	Forums; Book reviews; Adult fiction.
Geek in the Home	http://geekinthehome.wordpress.com	Book Reviews; New Products; Relationships; Wine/Winemaking; Recipes

Girl at a Startup	http://www.girlatastartup.com	Book Reviews; Celebrities; Comedy; Music; Regional; Regional General Interest; Entertainment
Joseph's Reviews	http://josephsreviews.wordpress.com	Book Reviews; Non-Fiction
Literary Mayhem	http://literarymayhem.com/wordpress	Book Reviews; Books
Long Beach Books Examiner	http://www.anovelquest.com	Book Reviews; Books
The Book Pushers	http://thebookpushers.com	Book Reviews; Books
The Quivering Pen	http://davidabramsbooks.blogspot.com	Book Reviews; Authors
Bookish	http://blogs.chron.com/bookish	Book Reviews; Books
Portland Book Review	http://www.portlandbookreview.com	Book Reviews; All Genres
Read Street	http://www.baltimoresun.com/features/books/read-street	Book Reviews; Books
Unshelved	http://www.unshelved.com	Book Reviews; Libraries
Rocky Mountain Reviews	http://www.rockymountainreviews.com	Book Reviews; All Genres

APPENDIX B

EBOOK PROMOTIONAL SITES

This is not an endorsement of these sites, but simply a compiled list of options based on my research.

Title	Website
Armadillo eBooks	http://www.armadilloebooks.com/submit-free-ebooks/
Author Marketing Club	http://authormarketingclub.com/members/submit-your-book/
Awesome Gang	http://awesomegang.com/submit-your-book/
Bargain Ebook Hunter	http://bargainebookhunter.com/feature-your-book/
Bargain eBook Hunter	http://bargainebookhunter.com/contact-us/
Book Angel	http://bookangel.co.uk/submit-your-book/
Book Deal Hunter	http://bookdealhunter.com/submit-free-book
Book Freebies	http://bookfreebies.com/submit-book.php
Book Goodies	http://bookgoodies.com/submit-your-free-kindle-days/
BookBub	www.bookbub.com
Christian Book Videos	www.christianbookvideos.com
Christian eBooks Today	http://www.christianebookstoday.com/advertising/free-fiction-nonfiction-lists/
Christian Kindle News	http://christiankindlenews.com/submit-kindle-deals/
ContentMo Free eBooks	http://contentmo.com/submit-your-free-ebook-promo

Daily Cheap Reads	http://dailycheapreads.com/your-two-cents-worth/
Deal Seeking Mom	http://dealseekingmom.com/about/contact
Digital Book Today	http://digitalbooktoday.com/12-top-100-submit-your-free-book-to-be-included-on-this-list/
eBook Booster	www.ebookbooster.com
eBook Deal of the Day	http://ebookdealofday.com/author-submit
eBook Deal of the Day UK	http://www.ebookdealoftheday.co.uk/submissions
Ebook Korner Kafe	http://kornerkonnection.com
eBookLister	http://www.ebooklister.net/submit.php
Ereader News Today	http://ereadernewstoday.com/ent-free-book-submissions/
eReaderPerks	http://www.ereaderperks.com/authors/
Free Digital Reads	http://freedigitalreads.com/author-submissions/
Free eBooks Blog	http://www.freeebooksblog.com/contact/
Freebies 4 Mom	http://freebies4mom.com/category/music-books/share-free-ebooks/?iframe=true
FreeBooks.com	http://www.freebooks.com/submit
Gospel eBooks	http://www.contactme.com/4efbf879ef17bb0001019490
Great Books Great Deals	http://greatbooksgreatdeals.wufoo.com/forms/z7x3p3/
Indie Book of the Day	http://indiebookoftheday.com/authors/free-on-kindle-listing/
Inspired Reads	http://www.inspiredreads.com/contact/
It's Write Now	http://www.itswritenow.com/submit-your-book

Jungle Deals and Steals	http://jungledealsandsteals.com/about/contact
Kindle Book Promos	http://kindlebookpromos.luckycinda.com/?page_id=283
Momma Says Read	http://www.mommasaysread.com/author-reviews/author-services
One Hundred Free eBooks	http://onehundredfreebooks.com/author-free-kindle-book-submission.html
Orangeberry Book Tours	https://docs.google.com/spreadsheet/viewform?formkey=dFEyLTFUSHREd05KaVItaDdUUkVVNGc6MA#gid=0
Pin Your Book	http://pinyourbook.com
Pixels of Ink	http://www.pixelofink.com/sfkb/
PixelScroll	http://pixelscroll.com/contact-us/
Super E-Books	http://super-e-books.com/how-to-add-your-free-e-book-to-the-super-e-books-calendar/
Sweeties Picks!	http://www.sweetiespicks.com/free-kindle-books
The Digital Ink Spot	https://docs.google.com/spreadsheet/embeddedform?formkey=dC1PcUFvVlZiV25lcjYtZzhtNzNQQnc6MQ
The eReader Cafe	http://www.theereadercafe.com/p/authors.html
Therese Heckenkamp Blog	http://www.thereseheckenkamp.com/more/free-christian-kindle-ebooks/authors-submit-your-free-ebook-promotion-here/
Your Daily Ebooks	http://www.yourdailyebooks.com/sample-page

APPENDIX C

FAIRS, TRADESHOWS, CONVENTIONS & CONFERENCES

American Library Association (ALA) Annual Conference

Arizona Daily Star Tucson Festival of Books with the University of Arizona (Tucson, AZ), Spring

Atlanta Journal-Constitution Decatur Book Festival, The (Atlanta, GA), Fall

Austin Book Festival (Austin, TX), Late Fall

Austin Jewish Community Book Fair, The (Austin, TX), Late Fall

Blackboard Festival (Houston, Texas)

Blue Metropolis (Montreal, CA), Spring

Bologna Children's Book Fair

BookExpo America, Spring

Brevard Authors Book Fair (Cocoa, FL), Spring

Brooklyn Book Festival (Brooklyn, NY), Fall

Buckeyes Book Fair (Wooster, OH), Late Fall

Celebrate the Book (Carlisle, PA), Fall

Central Coast Book and Author Festival (San Luis Obispo, CA), Fall

Christians In Action Tradeshow

Collingswood Book Festival (Collingswood, NJ), Fall

Connecticut Children's Book Fair (Storrs, CN), Fall

Delaware Book Festival (Dover, DE), Late Fall

Digital Book World Conference + Expo

Fall for the Book Literary Festival (Fairfax, VA), Fall

Frankfurt Book Fair (Germany)

Georgia Literary Festival, (Blue Ridge, GA), Fall

Great Salt Lake Book Fair

Hollywood Book Festival

Indianapolis Bookfest, Dolores Thornton, founder

International Christian Retail Show

Latino Book & Family Festivals, The

Litquake (San Francisco, CA), Fall

London Book Fair

Louisiana Book Festival (Baton Rouge, LA), Late Fall

Miami Book Fair International

Midwest Literary Festival (Aurora, IL), Fall

National Black Book Festival (Houston, TX)

Orange County Children's Book Festival (Costa Mesa, CA), Fall

Philadelphia Book Festival

Red Dirt Book Festival (Shawnee, Oklahoma)

Rochester Children's Book Festival (Rochester, NY), Late Fall

San Bernardino Book Fair at San Bernardino Valley College

Self-Publishing Book Expo

Spanish Christian Book Fair

Twin Cities Book Festival (Minneapolis, MN), Fall

Vegas Valley Book Festival (Las Vegas, NV), Fall

West Hollywood Book Fair

Wisconsin Book Festival (Madison, WI), Fall

Wordstock (Portland, OR), Late Fall

Wyoming Book Festival (Cheyenne, WY)

APPENDIX D

SAMPLE LETTERS & TEMPLATES

Book Review/ Author Interview Request Sample

Email Subject: THE INNER SOCIETY: New Novel Addresses Unspoken Teen Issues in Christian Literature

Dear _____,

Today's high schools are frightening battlegrounds of cyber bullying and gun violence. Teens are inundated by pop culture's contradicting messages about sexuality, religion, and success. Even when schools seem to be relatively positive environments, the powerful peer pressure to fit in can also cause many teens to be terrified of school.

In THE INNER SOCIETY (Ellechor Publishing House/March 2013), a new Christian Young Adult novel series by Melinda L. Bohannon, Norfolk High School in Virginia becomes the playground of a powerful society of rich and spoiled teenagers who believe they are inherently better than everyone else. That is, until Maggie Kraus, a rebellious and troubled teen, comes to Norfolk. When she blatantly challenges the balance of power, she becomes their next target. Will she survive the deadly game that follows?

Fans of the Twilight and Hunger Games trilogies, and any teen who has suffered adversity and heartbreak, will love the intense drama and suspense in Bohannon's new series of novels, based on the true lives and stories of teenagers the author encountered in her 20 years of dedication to teaching, youth advising, and foster parenting. Bohannon wrote the series with an intentionally secular tone, yet grounded the books in life-giving values so it could serve as a powerful tool for youth advisors and parents desperate to reach struggling teens who do not normally accept guidance from adults.

Drugs, pre-marital sex, abortion, pornography, and other timely issues often inadequately examined in Christian literature are carefully addressed through the experiences of the characters. In a recent interview Bohannon said, "If Christians won't get out of their comfort zones and venture out into the streets to reach teenagers in their own territory – they will not reach them at all." She hopes that THE INNER SOCIETY will inspire a new generation of writers who will not be afraid to deal with the heavy issues that teens face today in a world of rapidly declining values.

I would love to send you a copy of THE INNER SOCIETY for review consideration. Melinda Bohannon is also available for interviews.

Thanks for your consideration, and I look forward to hearing from you.

About Melinda Bohannon:

A graduate of California State University, Fullerton, Melinda Bohannon has worked as a teacher and lecturer for nearly 20 years, mostly dealing with troubled teenagers, foster children, parent/child recovery groups, and special education. She grew up in the Bay Area, but now resides in Fresno County with her husband Richard, two sons, and adopted daughter in Sanger, CA. For more info, visit www.7rain7.com.

About Ellechor Publishing House:

The traditional publishing imprint of Ellechor Media, Ellechor Publishing is an award-winning small press that has published over 20 Christian publications since its official launch in 2011. Our titles have won various awards, including the 2011 Genesis Award, 2011 Genesis double Semi-Finalists, a 2010 Daphne Finalist, a 2nd place Orange County Christian Writers Conference Award in May 2010, and a 2007 Golden Palm Finalist Award.

- A proud winner of the September 2010 Most Loved Business Award from Intuit's Love a Local Business campaign, Ellechor Publishing House is distributed to the trade by Advocate Distribution Solutions (STL) and is a member of the following associations:

- CBA, the Association for Christian Retail

- Christian Small Publishers Association, CSPA

- Recognized Publisher, American Christian Fiction Writers

Regards,

ROCHELLE CARTER

CEO/ Publisher

Ellechor Media, LLC

Endorsement Request Template

Dear John Doe,

I was wondering if you'd be able to help me.

I'm getting ready to have my latest book, **TITLED**, published on **LAUNCH DATE**. It [*include a brief summary of what makes your book interesting here. No more than 2-3 lines*].

Being a big fan of your work, [*this is where you schmooze! Explain why you chose them in particular and how what they do ties to you and your book*].

So, I would like to send you a complimentary advance review copy of my book and, if you like it, would like to invite you to write an endorsement. My publisher estimates initial sales to be in the region of xxx - xxx [*only include this if you know your estimated reach. Leave it out if you do not know.*], so it would give you further exposure with readers interested in [*whatever the two of you have in common*], while I get the acclaim of having my book endorsed by a respected [*what they do goes here*].

If you could just let me know if you'd like to take a look then I'll email you a copy immediately for your review and potential endorsement.

Best regards,

ROCHELLE CARTER

ADDITIONAL RESOURCES

It is highly recommended that you to seek out additional resources to gain a more in-depth knowledge about the writing, editing, publishing, and marketing processes so that you can be as educated as possible. Since you are planning a serious career as an authorpreneur, consider the following additional reading:

Writing

- *Outlining Your Novel* by K. M. Weiland

- *Structuring Your Novel* by K. M. Weiland

- *On Writing Well*, 30th Anniversary Edition: The Classic Guide to Writing Nonfiction by William Zinsser

Editing

- *Self-Editing for Fiction Writers, Second Edition: How to Edit Yourself Into Print* by Renni Browne and Dave King

- *Editor-Proof Your Writing: 21 Steps to the Clear Prose Publishers and Agents Crave* by Don McNair
- *Revision and Self Editing for Publication: Techniques for Transforming Your First Draft into a Novel that Sells* by James Scott Bell

Publishing

- *The Self-Publishing Manual* by Dan Poynter
- *Putting Your Passion Into Print: Get Your Book Published Successfully!* by Arielle Eckstut and David Sterry

Marketing

- *The Frugal Book Promoter* by Carolyn Howard-Johnson
- *Plug Your Book!: Online Book Marketing for Authors* by Steve Weber
- *1001 Ways to Market Your Books (1001 Ways to Market Your Books: For Authors and Publishers)* by John Kremer

ACKNOWLEDGEMENTS

First and foremost, I need to thank God for providing me with the opportunity to build my businesses and care for my family.

Thank you and I love you to my biggest supporters: my husband Al-Tajuan, my sister Andrea, and my mother Sylvia. I would not be here today if it were not for their commitment to my success, their support in every way needed, their acceptance of my goals, and their ability to motivate me (aka annoy me until I do something) when I get lazy like no other.

Thank you from the bottom of my heart to the staff, editors, and graphic designers who have been with Ellechor from the beginning, and to those who have sacrificed personal gain to allow us to grow. My sister Alvetta Rolle, author of *The Mercy Seat* and *Potiphar's Wife*, my company's branding genius, Caroll Atkins of C.A. Sly Designs, Doug West with Zaq Designs, my senior editor, Veronika Walker of InkWork Services, editor Emily Sather, and Steve Plummer, graphic designer extraordinaire at SP Designs, Olson Perry Sr., and Lady Dana Austin are just a few of the wonderful people who have journeyed with us.

Last, but certainly not least, thank you to all of the 30+ Ellechor Media authors who have entrusted me with their written visions. It has been a blessing, a learning opportunity, and a reminder of whom I serve: God, family, and my authors.

ABOUT THE AUTHOR

ROCHELLE CARTER IS the CEO of Ellechor Media, LLC and the author of *The 7-Step Guide To Authorpreneurship* (EverFaith Press, 2014), *Write Success: Inspirational Quotes For The Authorpreneur* (EverFaith Press, 2013), and *Three Hour Heels: A Novel* (Ellechor Publishing House, 2015). She has received national recognition for her leadership and professional achievements as a finalist in the Entrepreneur of the Year (Creative Arts & Media) and Business on the Rise categories of the 2014 Stiletto Women In Business Award (SWIBA) competition, and again as a Woman of Outstanding Leadership by The International Women's Leadership Association.

A board member for Women Entrepreneurs of Oregon and Portland's Leadership and Entrepreneurship Public Charter High School, Carter is also an Authorpreneur Business Consultant, providing publishing consulting services for various authors, and managing the acquisition and production process for all of her imprints.

Through her award-winning company, she publishes books and magazines with a purpose, going beyond the realm of simple entertainment by seeking to enlighten and uplift readers. Her imprints have published over 40 books in less than three years, 98% of which enjoy 4-star or higher Amazon ratings. She resides in Portland with her husband and two children.

About the Company:

Ellechor Media, LLC (www.ellechormedia.com) is comprised of two Christian publishing imprints and one self-publishing imprint, all of which are currently distributed to the trade by Advocate Distribution Solutions, a division of Send the Light (STL). Ellechor Media is a proud member of the Independent Book Publishers Association (IBPA).

- Ellechor Publishing House, LLC (www. ellechorpublishinghouse.com) – A traditional, royalty-paying imprint. Named Intuit's Most Loved Local Business by popular vote in September 2010, Ellechor Publishing is currently a recognized publisher with American Christian Fiction Writer's Association, and a member of the Christian Small Publishers Association (CSPA).

- EverFaith Press (www.everfaithpress.com) – A self-publishing imprint for businesses and authors of inspirational fiction and nonfiction.

The team also offers stand-alone marketing services for authors of all genres.

- Ellechor eBooks & Co. (www.e2books.co) – Ellechor's newest imprint, focusing on electronic book production. Ellechor eBooks & Co. is a royalty-paying, e-book-only publishing imprint. e2Books cooperatively markets its eBooks with other Ellechor Media titles.

Made in the USA
Columbia, SC
08 August 2019